HOW TO FAIL
AS A THERAPIST

PUBLISHER'S NOTE

This publication is designed to provide accurate and authoritative information in regard to the subject matter covered. It is sold with the understanding that the publisher is not engaged in rendering psychological, medical, or other professional service.

Books in The Practical Therapist Series® *present authoritative answers to the question, "What-do-I-do-now-and-how-do-I-do-it?" in the practice of psychotherapy, bringing the wisdom and experience of expert mentors to the practicing therapist. A book, however, is no substitute for thorough professional training and adherence to ethical and legal standards. At minimum:*

- ➤ *The practitioner must be qualified to practice psychotherapy.*
- ➤ *Clients participate in psychotherapy only with informed consent.*
- ➤ *The practitioner must not "guarantee" a specific outcome.*

— Robert E. Alberti, Ph.D., Editor

Other Titles in The Practical Therapist Series®

HOW TO FAIL
AS A THERAPIST

50 WAYS TO LOSE OR
DAMAGE YOUR PATIENTS

BERNARD SCHWARTZ, PH.D.
JOHN V. FLOWERS, PH.D.

FOREWORD BY ARNOLD A. LAZARUS, PH.D., ABPP

Impact 🐚 *Publishers*®
ATASCADERO, CALIFORNIA

ATTENTION ORGANIZATIONS AND CORPORATIONS:
This book is available at quantity discounts on bulk purchases for educational, business, or sales promotional use. For further information, please contact Impact Publishers, P.O. Box 6016, Atascadero, California 93423-6016. Phone: 805-466-5917, e-mail: info@impactpublishers.com

Library of Congress Cataloging-in-Publication Data

Schwartz, Bernard, 1943-
    How to fail as a therapist : 50 ways to lose or damage your patients / Bernard Schwartz and John V. Flowers.
        p. ; cm.
    Includes bibliographical references and index.
    ISBN 1-886230-70-6 (alk. paper)
    1. Psychotherapy. 2. Psychotherapy patients. 3. Psychotherapist and patient. 4. Mental health services—Utilization.
    [DNLM: 1. Psychotherapy—methods. 2. Professional-Patient Relations. WM 420 S399h 2006] I. Flowers, John V., 1938- II. Title.
    RC480.5.S33 2006
    616.89'14—dc22

                                                            2006002040

Impact Publishers and colophon are registered trademarks of Impact Publishers, Inc.

Cover design by Gayle Downs, Gayle Force Design, Atascadero, California.
Composition by UB Communications, Parsippany, New Jersey.
Printed in the United States of America on acid-free, recycled paper.
Published by **Impact 🕮 Publishers®**
POST OFFICE BOX 6016
ATASCADERO, CALIFORNIA 93423-6016
www.impactpublishers.com

Dedication

To those clients, clinicians and researchers whose insights illuminate these pages.

— Bernard Schwartz
— John V. Flowers

Contents

Contents

Foreword

There is a slippery underbelly to the successful practice of psychotherapy that is almost never taught in graduate programs or medical schools. In fact, it is rarely mentioned. Core curricula in psychology, psychiatry, counseling, and social work focus on various theories, research protocols, assessment instruments, psychometric procedures, counseling methods, and clinical techniques but have little to offer when it comes to nitty-gritty therapeutic decisions. Stated differently, it may be said that insufficient formal attention is paid to the artistry involved in managing interviews and dealing with minor lapses or oversights that may rupture relationships.

I have lost count of how many brilliant graduate students had studied for years, gained A+ grades in all their courses, but lacked any clear idea of how to talk to a client. They had acquired massive amounts of data pertaining to theoretical underpinnings, emerged well versed in the writings of innumerable experts, were filled to capacity with opinions and beliefs, especially after viewing hours of putative master clinicians on tape but were left with gaping holes in the niceties of client management. With panicky undertones they would ask: "What do I say for starters?" "Are there some good icebreakers?" In an engaging manner, Drs. Bernard Schwartz and John Flowers have filled these lacunae with numerous clues, strategies, and precise interventions gleaned mainly from the research on clinical effectiveness and their own clinical experience.

I shudder when I think back to 1960 when I, as a newly minted Ph.D. in clinical psychology, was certified as competent and qualified to set up a private practice and stepped into my freshly furnished office ready to minister to those in need of psychotherapeutic assistance. From the vantage point of almost four dozen years of retrospective acumen, it is not farfetched to say that I knew next to nothing. There was very little I could take into my consulting room from the dry academic bones I had to collect or from the metaphorical intellectual hurdles I had to jump over to get there. Perhaps the best piece of advice I received was from a supervisor during one of my internship rotations at a day hospital in London. "Be yourself," he said, "but examine your feelings." In other words, don't be a slave to some strict theory, don't just go by the book, trust your intuition but not without questioning it, and remember to keep your brain in gear.

While reading the page proofs of this book, I wondered what impact perusing a copy in 1960 would have had on my career. Certainly many skills, therapeutic tactics and answers to clinical conundrums that had to be acquired the hard way, by trial and error, would have enhanced my clinical repertoire almost immediately. It would have enabled me to construct a trajectory to bypass many obstacles and sidestep pitfalls. And so it is with anyone who reads the book in present time — elusive clinical pieces of wisdom are handed to you on a platter! Not that I agree with everything in the book. But that's the best part — it stimulates you to think. And Drs. Schwartz and Flowers have obviously done a lot of creative thinking and reading and experimenting to have produced such a useful book. If you treat, coach, or counsel people or engage in clinical supervision, it will make your work a lot easier and more effective.

— Arnold A. Lazarus, Ph.D., ABPP
Distinguished Professor Emeritus of Psychology,
    Rutgers University and
Executive Director of The Lazarus Institute,
    Skillman, New Jersey

Introduction

In a recent book "master therapists" were asked to relate one example of a therapeutic error they had made in their career. In response, one noted clinician confided that it was nearly impossible to cite just one example, since he made numerous mistakes every day.

— W. Glasser (2002)

Depending on which study you read, between 20 and 57% of patients do not return after their initial session. Another 37 to 45% only attend therapy a total of two times.

— D. G. Cross and C. E. Warren (1984)

Let's see, high therapy dropout rates on the one hand and a high frequency of therapist errors on the other... It doesn't take a Ph.D. in clinical psychology to suspect a connection between these two factors. In fact, clients[1] often cite dissatisfaction with their therapists as the reason for early termination of therapy (Acosta, 1980; Cross & Warren, 1984; Hynan, 1990). And, those clients who drop out early display poor treatment outcomes, overutilize mental health services, and demoralize clinicians. Quite a flow chart — from client dissatisfaction to dropping out, to poor outcomes, to demoralized clinicians who may need therapy themselves. . . .

Worse yet, a follow-up study on dropouts (the technical term is *unilateral terminators*) found that most clinicians had no idea why their patients had terminated or thought they were satisfied

---

[1] Although the term *client* is preferable, we also use *patient* interchangeably throughout this book to avoid redundancy.

terminators. However, their clients could define very specific "therapeutic errors" or therapist deficits such as feeling uncomfortable talking to their therapists (Hynan, 1990). The conclusion is that we therapists are as adept at denial, deception, and rationalization (depending on your school of thought) as our clients.

Now the good news (after all, therapy should be optimistic): there are a number of well-researched strategies that have been proven to reduce dropout rates and increase positive treatment outcomes. For example, in one study a simple phone call to confirm a client's first appointment resulted in a two-thirds reduction in dropouts. Unfortunately, it is often labor intensive to seek out and review much of the relevant research because it is scattered throughout the literature — a journal article here, a chapter in a book there. And unfortunately, most mental health clinicians, with and without a Ph.D., rate reading research as a very low clinical priority.

Thus, a major task in writing this book was to assemble, organize, and condense the vast body of research addressing therapeutic effectiveness. We feel passionately that treatment decisions should be based on the best available scientific research. Too often in the past this has not been the case. For example, during the last century, quite a few "renowned" experts concluded that mothers were to blame for a host of childhood emotional disorders: autism was allegedly caused by detached "refrigerator mothers," asthma by smothering mothers, and schizophrenia by mothers sending "double-bind" messages.

These unfounded ideas had no scientific support whatsoever but were based on personal experience, good old "common sense," and a healthy dose of megalomania — with the result that untold numbers of parents suffered unnecessary guilt for decades until research unveiled the biological bases of these and a number of other emotional disorders.

We begin our exploration of the fifty most common therapeutic errors by addressing the early stages of therapy. In chapter I, How to Fail Even Before You Start Therapy, we examine how clinicians often fail to examine their clients' expectations and how this results in negative therapeutic outcomes. Chapter II, How to Perform Incomplete Assessments, discusses frequently overlooked clinical factors such as the client's "stage-of-change" and "psychological reactance," both of which can greatly impact treatment decisions. Next, in chapter III, How to Ignore Science, we identify various factors that prevent therapists from reliance on scientifically researched treatment protocols.

One of the most researched areas in psychotherapy involves the construction of the therapist-client "working alliance." In chapter IV, How to Avoid Collaboration with the Client, and chapter V, How to Ruin the Therapist-Client Relationship, we investigate the clinical errors that cause many clients to feel "uncared for" in spite of their therapist's best attempts to express warmth and empathy. We also identify common therapist errors made when seeking and responding to client feedback about the therapeutic relationship. Chapter VI, How to Set Improper Therapist-Client Boundaries, analyzes boundary errors such as overidentification or fusion with the client, overly rigid boundaries, and inappropriate therapist disclosure.

In chapters VII through XI, we examine therapeutic errors made during the treatment process itself. These include How to Guarantee Noncompliance with Assignments, How to Make Bad Attitudes Worse, How Not to Confront Clients, How to Get Clients to Refuse Medication, and How Not to Terminate Therapy.

Chapter XII, How to Achieve Therapist Burnout, describes the "inner world" of the therapist and the need for appropriate "self-care" for those in the helping professions. Clinicians can become so immersed in the lives of others, "their hopes, ideas, goals, aspirations, pains, fears, despair, anger. . . " (Rogers, 1995) that we can lose sight of our own needs. And, without proper "self-care," clinicians are unlikely to be as patient, nurturing, and positive as is required of therapists. As Carl Rogers, the father of humanistic psychology, stated toward the end of his career, "I have always been better at caring and looking after others than caring for myself. But in these later years, I have made progress" (Rogers, 1995).

In speaking about therapeutic errors, Arnold Lazarus, one of the major innovators in the field, recently described his work with postdoctoral students, "We often discuss blunders we have made, why we should not hide them, and what we can learn from these mistakes" (Lazarus, 2002). Unfortunately, too many therapists do not accept, let alone reflect on, their fallibility. Thus we conclude this introduction by presenting what we consider to be the first and fundamental therapeutic error: failing to recognize our limitations as therapists. (Each therapeutic error described in this book is followed by a section titled, Avoiding the Error, which offers practical strategies to improve clinical effectiveness.)

 ## *Error #1*

Failing to Recognize Our Limitations as Therapists

The difference between good and bad mothers is not in the commission of errors, it is what they do with them.

— D. W. Winnicott (1997)

One of the major ways of learning is through mistakes. They provide clues for further growth.

— A. Lazarus (1977)

After years and years of study, comprehensive exams, postgraduate supervision, and licensing exams, it is quite natural for those of us in the mental health field to feel that we have (or should have) all of the answers to clinical matters — that we should never slip up. Thus, when patients voice their concerns about their progress or, worse yet, when they drop out or deteriorate under our care, there is a tendency to avoid accepting responsibility for committing a possible therapeutic error. It is easier to point the finger elsewhere — "maybe the problems were too severe, the patient was not ready or willing to change, the problem was biological." These explanations, even when partially valid, protect us from engaging in a process of self-reflection or an exploration of what might have gone wrong in a particular case.

Dr. Mentor, a supervisor in a Ph.D. program at a prestigious university, was meeting with a colleague and mentioned that "one of his interns was having great difficulty with a case." This client was obsessing about his "impure" thoughts, thoughts that he felt were sinful and might result in dire spiritual consequences for him. Standard treatment for obsessiveness was not working, and in fact the client's condition was worsening. The colleague made a suggestion that the supervisor found to be quite useful. A short time later, the supervisor confessed to the colleague who had made the suggestion that the "obsesser" was actually one of his own cases, not that of an intern. He stated, "I am supposed to be an expert on obsessive-compulsive problems — and I was too embarrassed to admit I needed help."

In this case, even though Dr. Mentor used a little subterfuge in the process, he was able to admit to himself that he needed input on his difficult case, and this resulted in his being a more effective clinician.

This book is based on the premise that all of us will experience failure at one time or another in our practices. Some patients will terminate unexpectedly, others will justifiably complain of lack of progress, still others will baffle us. We may be late to a session, make an error in billing, or even schedule two patients for the same hour. There is seemingly no way around our fallibility other than denial — and we know as therapists what the consequences of denial are.

Accepting our fallibility has several beneficial effects. It keeps us humble by reminding us we don't have all the answers. Awareness of our imperfections can also drive us toward improving our skills by keeping up with the literature, consulting with colleagues, and participating in workshops for the joy of learning and not just for continuing education credit. Acceptance also relieves us of several burdens: we no longer have to come up with elaborate excuses for blunders (the client or circumstances are to blame), we can relinquish our feelings of guilt (we are not supposed to be perfect), and we can feel free to admit to our mistakes to ourselves, colleagues, and clients.

❖ Avoiding the Error

1. Engage in the same cognitive interventions with yourself that you would use with a client. For example, if a client terminates prematurely, you might feel awful at first. However, you could compare your "termination" rate with the norm, which as mentioned earlier in this chapter can reach as high as fifty

percent. Hopefully, when you consider all of the data, your successes, and your failures, you will find that your success rate is better than average. If not, then perhaps it would be appropriate for you to employ one or more of the self-assessment tools included in this book.

2. Inform a trusted colleague when you feel that you made an error with a client. Revealing your imperfections gets easier over time and reduces their power, and your colleagues will respect you for your honesty and self-reflection.

3. Remember Carl Jung's maxim: "Perfection is the enemy of the good." To counter perfectionist thinking when it comes to failure, ask yourself, "What is likely to happen as a result of this failure?" You can also apply Arnold Lazarus's "six-month rule" by asking yourself, "In six months will I even remember this event?"

As we reviewed the literature on the traits of "master therapists," we found that one characteristic they seemed to have in common was that of humility — the recognition of their own limitations. As one respected clinician put it, "Bad therapists don't know what they don't know" (Jennings, Sovereign, & Bottorff, 2005). We hope this book serves as a reminder that we are all works in progress.

How to Fail Even Before You Start Therapy

A recent comprehensive review of motion pictures found that in the last decade, psychologists were portrayed in over 1500 films. Unfortunately, only 20% of those films featured competent, effective or ethical clinicians. Instead therapists are often evildoers (Silence of the Lambs); *hysterical and unethical* (Deconstructing Harry); *or merely incompetent* (Lethal Weapon I, II, III, IV).

— J. V. Flowers and P. Frizler (2004)

We are living in an age in which the general population has become more and more accepting of psychotherapy as a useful and appropriate tool to use in coping with life's challenges. However, when new clients arrive for their first session, they bring with them a myriad of expectations and conceptions about the therapy process. Some of these may be realistic — others may not. For example, those who have been exposed to talk show therapists may expect that their problems will be addressed and resolved instantaneously. Others may expect that therapy is like visiting the family physician — where you describe your symptoms and the doctor tells you what the diagnosis is and what to do about it, a kind of a "take two aspirin and stay out of drafts" concept of psychotherapy. In reality, approximately two-thirds of new clients have little or no idea about what therapy entails. According to Strupp and Bloxom (1973)

> Adequate preparation (for therapy) has been associated with numerous positive therapy outcomes including: increased motivation and expectations of improvement; viewing the therapist as more interested,

respectful and accepting; decreased approval seeking behavior and a better understanding of the therapy process and their role in it.

As the research cited above indicates, there are numerous benefits to providing information about the process of therapy to clients. However, often this crucial component of treatment is minimized — or overlooked altogether.

Error #2

Failing to Address Client Expectations about Therapy

> A client with panic attacks was asked how long she thought would be required to resolve the problem. With a deep sigh she answered, "I hope it won't take too many years." When the therapist replied that such problems are typically resolved within several months, she was wide eyed with surprise.

Nearly all therapists provide an information packet that addresses such issues as financial responsibilities, cancelled appointment policies, limits to confidentiality, and emergency procedures. However, it is equally important to assess the client's preconceived ideas of what therapy entails so that any misconceptions can be addressed. One example of a quite thorough printed statement of practices and procedures to inform clients may be found at *http://www.horizonscounseling.com/Forms/licensed.PDF.*

The problem is that although organizational, bookkeeping, and legal matters are the same for every client, and therefore easy to address, clients may have a variety of expectations about the therapeutic process itself that needs to be assessed on an individual basis. One common misconception involves the amount of time clients believe may be necessary to resolve their problems. As the case above involving panic attacks illustrates, some clients believe their problems may require much longer to resolve than is typical. At the other extreme are those overly optimistic (somewhat deluded) folk with serious and complex problems who believe in the "quick fix." Such was the case of a chronic problem drinker whose job, marriage, and health were at risk but who thought that "a couple of sessions" would be all that was necessary. In actuality, it took nearly two sessions just to prioritize his goals and provide education about the nature and pacing of personal change.

Clients also may have distorted ideas about the process of therapy itself. Thus, it is helpful to ask toward the end of the first session whether what went on was what they expected.

> Jason, age 45, suffered from severe stress responses to a variety of public situations, such as dinner parties, business meetings, and the like. He was particularly concerned about the embarrassment caused by his excessive sweating and flushing on these occasions. At the conclusion of the first session, when queried about whether his expectations of therapy were met, he wondered why the therapist was not focusing more on his family of origin where "the problem was caused in the first place." Following this acknowledgment, a discussion ensued describing the difference between "solution-based approaches" and those that involve resolving historical issues.

In this particular case, Jason was relieved to hear that his issues could be resolved somewhat rapidly. However, some clients may prefer a different treatment option. At such times clients can be asked whether they would like a referral to a therapist they might match up better with.

❖ Avoiding the Error

1. Leave an appropriate amount of time toward the end of the first session to assess whether the client's expectations have been met. At this time the following issues can be addressed: the importance of therapist-client collaboration, the therapist's general approach to dealing with the type of problem presented by the client, a general time frame for the length of treatment, and the concept that ending therapy (termination) is something that should be a mutual decision.

2. If clients have not had previous therapy experience, investigate whether descriptions of therapy from friends or the media have influenced their expectations about therapy. Respond to any inaccurate expectations they might have developed.

A case in point involved a client whose grown daughter had allegedly "recovered memories" of him having abused her as a young child. During an extensive assessment of all relevant historical information, he interrupted the therapist to ask, "When are you going to hypnotize me to find out if her allegations are true?" Obviously, he had expectations derived from the media or acquaintances, and these needed to be addressed early in the session so that the client and therapist could get on the same page. As it turned out, the therapist explained that hypnosis was not necessarily reliable when it came to obtaining historical information. However, because of the client's expectations of how therapy should proceed, he cancelled his next appointment and stated he was seeking someone who had an expertise in hypnosis.

3. Expectations can and should be addressed on a regular basis in order to assess whether patient expectations have changed or new expectations that were not identified earlier have arisen.

Error #3

Failing to Inspect the Client's Previous Experience with Psychotherapy

Scott presented for therapy with what seemed to be a typical "fear of flying" phobia. However, a review of his prior therapy experience revealed that he had already been treated for this disorder with a complete desensitization protocol, which had not been successful, and also had been treated for post-traumatic stress disorder related to his son's death from a drug overdose. This information, as painful as it was to relate, was crucial for developing an appropriate treatment plan.

Without a meticulous inspection of prior treatment, therapy could have been fruitless in this case at best and damaging at worst. It can also be useful to find out if the client felt the previous therapist committed any errors during the course of therapy. The questions "What was most helpful?" and "What was less helpful or bothersome" can help you avoid repeating the same mistakes as the previous therapist. For example, one client complained that the therapist took too many notes during the session. Interestingly, other clients have stated concerns about therapists who rarely took notes and seemed not to remember specific events discussed in previous sessions. "To each his own" — in life and in therapy.

❖ Avoiding the Error

1. Review the client's previous therapy experiences with a variety of questions including
   a. How long did the therapy last?
   b. How did it end?
   c. How was your relationship with the therapist?
   d. What was the best part of the experience? The worst part?
   e. What do you wish you had done differently in the sessions?
   f. How might you be different entering treatment at this time than you were the last time?

2. Consider how clients' answers might affect their views and expectations of therapy.
   a. Get a sense of whether the client thought that the previous therapy moved at a comfortable pace or whether it felt rushed or not dynamic enough. This information can aid in constructing an appropriately paced treatment plan.
   b. Inspect how the previous therapy was terminated. For example, a client who terminated by simply calling and canceling one day is likely to do that again. To avoid this scenario, inform clients that the end of therapy can be as important as the beginning and request that they participate in a "summary" session if at all possible before terminating.
   c. Assess the quality of the relationship with the previous therapist. Such information can be helpful by raising "red flags" about what might be problematic in establishing the working alliance. For example, a client may report having often felt anger at the previous therapist. Being forewarned about this possibility allows the therapist to prepare for the recurrence of similar feelings.

❖ *Error #4*

Failing to Explain the Therapist's Expectations Regarding the Therapeutic Process

After having spent the entire session discussing, planning, and strategizing how to improve a client's marriage, the client rises and announces that she moved out of the house and is filing for divorce.

The session ends and the client mentions that he was arrested for a DUI — and won't be able to attend the next meeting.

"Doorknob disclosures" such as those described above and other impediments to effective use of therapy sessions can be avoided if clinicians clearly describe their expectations in the early stages of therapy (or at any point when the direction of therapy changes). Of course these expectations may differ depending on the therapist's orientation and involve a wide range of attitudes and behaviors that might include the following:

a. Expectations regarding the role of "out-of-session" assignments.
b. The setting of appropriate therapist-client boundaries.
c. The need for active participation by the client in session agendas and the direction of treatment.
d. The need for therapy to be interactive, with neither party engaging in monologues.
e. The specific therapeutic interventions, such as dream interpretation or hypnosis, employed by the therapist.

❖Avoiding the Error

1. Inform clients that their ongoing input is essential and that they should be assertive in letting the therapist know whenever they feel that the therapist is "off track" in what is being focused on or with treatment recommendations.

   For example, in one case a therapist was so intent on following up with material from a previous session that he didn't check to see if any new issues had occurred since the last session. His client, who had been "empowered" by the therapist, was able to say, "Doctor what you are addressing is important, but right now it is far more crucial to address the fight I had with my boss which has led to a suspension."

2. When a "doorknob disclosure" is made, reassure the client that the topic will definitely be taken up at the next session, and also state that it is important to bring up important issues as early as possible in sessions so that an appropriate amount of time can be devoted to them. In fact it is a good idea to include this in your orientation of clients.

3. Inform the client that therapy works best if after discussing all pressing issues, the client is helped to prioritize so that no more than two or three problems are on the table at the same time. Obviously crisis issues must be addressed as they arise.

❖ *Error #5*

Failing to Prepare Clients for the Variety of Emotions That Therapy Can Evoke

A male client in his late twenties spent the first session letting his intern therapist "get to know him" by going into inordinate detail of his early life, his education, and his various travels. In session two, he continued his memoirs but became more and more agitated as he started to describe an event in which he had been sexually assaulted. At this point he became inconsolable, expressing great anger and shame and stating that he felt that this experience had ruined his ability to have intimate relationships. Try as she might, the therapist had extreme difficulty reducing the emotional eruption; and although another appointment was made for the next day, the client never returned to therapy nor would he return the therapist's follow-up calls.

Many clients expect therapy to elicit strong emotions and are not troubled by this idea. These "discloser-types" have vast experience sharing their emotions and are reasonably comfortable with negative feelings. On the other hand, as was illustrated by the case cited above, there are a number of clients who can be highly distressed by the intensity of their emotional responses to personal disclosure and negative memories. These clients typically fall into three categories:

1. Highly controlled individuals who have "shut down" — or are unaware of — their feelings.

2. Those who have learned to distract themselves from strong emotions.

3. Clients who are reserved in their emotional expression and generally unassertive. This is the group of clients that needs substantial preparation for exploration of strong negative feelings.

❖ Avoiding the Error

Carefully assess your clients to determine where they lie on the spectrum from discloser to nondiscloser. In the case above, the client was highly verbal but tended not to disclose emotionally laden issues. During the second session, he began to move toward disclosure and the therapist should have been more proactive when noticing increased agitation as the story unfolded by having the client slow down, taking a break perhaps, and then carefully assessing to see whether the client was ready to deal with the highly volatile material.

1. Be alert to signs that a client may be highly vulnerable to emotional disclosures:
   a. Statements such as "I've never told anyone this before."
   b. Fluid wording when talking about nonpersonal issues, but halting or choppy word flow when the topics become more personal.
   c. A tendency to self-distract when speaking of personal issues.
   d. A rolling autobiography that "needs" to be told in a logical or chronological fashion.
   e. Nonverbal signs such as eyes tearing up, nervous facial or hand gestures, and restlessness.

2. Prepare all clients for the fact that many uncomfortable emotions have to be experienced more than once to be resolved. Some clients have an attitude that likens therapy to a

physical workout — that is, "no pain, no gain." These clients need to be "slowed down" with reminders that it takes time to heal and that therapy is not a competitive sport.

❖ *Error #6*

Failing to Enhance Client Expectations of Success

In Interpersonal Psychotherapy for depression (IPT) patients are told at the very beginning of treatment that the "outlook for your recovery is excellent and you are going to be actively engaged in therapy."

— G. Klerman (1984)

Another "curative" factor that has received a good deal of scientific research is the effect of positive patient expectations on outcome in therapy. When clients have hope instilled in them at the outset of therapy, it is likely to increase their "active engagement" in the therapeutic process, which in turn leads to greater improvement (Meyer et al., 2002). Of course expectations for improvement need to be reasonable in relation to the extent of the clients' problems and the amount of treatment they have previously undergone. Raising false hopes can be as injurious to the therapeutic process as not engendering sufficient hope.

Positive expectations actually enhance the "real" effectiveness of interventions by decreasing depression, feelings of helplessness, hopelessness, and lowered energy. Such expectations help create their own success. In addition, the mysterious placebo effect is strengthened by positive expectations. Of course, no client should be promised or guaranteed resolution of the problem. Even though we know which approaches are likely to help specific problems, "likelihood" does not equate to "absolutes."

❖ Avoiding the Error

1. Assess the client's level of positive expectations by asking the question "What do you think is likely to happen as a result of your treatment." If the client's expectations are low, the therapist should convey that others with similar problems have

made significant progress and have enhanced the quality of their lives because of what they have learned in therapy.

2. Apply the "baby steps" rule when attempting to modify a client's expectations. That is, the new, more adaptive attitude should be only slightly different from the attitude the client currently holds. For example, it would be counterproductive to suggest to highly reserved and anxious individuals that therapy will transform them. However, it would be reasonable to suggest that most clients who seek help for anxiety "become more comfortable overall" and handle difficult situations more confidently.

❖ *Error #7*

Failing to Understand How Our Assumptions Affect Therapeutic Practices

Our tacit assumptions about human nature unquestionably influence how we view and serve individuals who seek psychological services.

— M. J. Mahoney (1991)

A new patient is about to enter your office. You know nothing about this person, and thus when you first meet you have no preconceptions — he or she is a blank slate awaiting your impressions. True? Actually, nothing could be further from the truth. Beginning in childhood, we develop a lot of underlying assumptions about human nature that we are often not aware of but that can affect how we view and deal with our loved ones, friends, colleagues, and clients.

Several assumptions that can affect clinical practice were identified by Wrightsman (1992). As you examine each category, it can be illuminating to reflect on your own assumptions about human nature.

1. Trustworthiness vs. Untrustworthiness — Are people basically trustworthy? Those of us who feel that adults and even children are basically trustworthy will approach therapy quite differently than those with the opposite belief. For example, as clinicians

we might recommend greater monitoring and supervision than is warranted if we feel that people are not worthy of trust.

2. Strength of Personal Will vs. External Control — Are people responsible for their problems, or can external factors contribute significantly to the difficulties we face in life? If we believe that people totally create their own destinies, we might be prone to overpathologize our clients and to not be sufficiently empathetic to the vagaries of human experience.

3. Altruism vs. Selfishness — Are people mainly out for themselves, or do they often demonstrate deep concern for the well-being of others? Clinicians who view people as essentially self-centered will view client behavior differently than those who consider the possibility that a client's actions may be motivated by concern for others. The assumption that people are out for themselves would affect how and where a clinician encourages a client to look for social support. For example, a client who had little social contact beyond her family moved to a new location due to her husband's job transfer. She had adequate social skills but did not build new friendships, largely because she was overly cautious in disclosing any significant information about herself. At first the therapist addressed the issue of self-disclosure, as if she needed skill building in this area. However, the real problem was her near total lack of trust in people, stemming from bad experiences in the small town from which she came.

4. Complexity vs. Simplicity — Are human beings easy to understand, or are we complicated and not easy to define with diagnostic categories and labels? If the actions and lives of people can be reduced to a simple formula, there can be a tendency to employ "formulistic" approaches to all presenting problems, without allowing for individual differences.

One of the most potent assumptions for clinicians about human nature is whether we believe human beings can change significantly. Those of us who believe that only minor changes can be expected, particularly with certain types of clients, may find that a self-fulfilling prophecy occurs in which our lowered expectations are reflected in the types of treatment protocols we attempt. In practice, pessimism about clients such as sex offenders, recalcitrant substance abusers, and others who come to therapy involuntarily has been shown to dramatically affect therapeutic outcome (Garb, 1996).

Recognizing the power of our personal assumptions is a first step. Next, we must carefully examine those assumptions to uncover overgeneralizations and invalid stereotypes.

❖Avoiding the Error

1. After reviewing the assumptions of human nature discussed above, assess whether there is a tendency for you to view human nature as primarily selfish, untrustworthy, simplistic, or difficult to change. If so, reflect on those individuals you have dealt with who have exhibited different behavioral tendencies.

2. Examine your emotional reactions to strangers. This technique seems particularly useful for discerning implicit assumptions one may have about classes of people, such as persons of a different gender, race, or age group.

3. Learn from your difficult cases. For example, one clinician who worked with personality-disordered clients realized he had been assuming that these clients are satisfied with their lifestyles and choose to maintain their behavior. Upon reflection, however, he developed a more therapeutic assumption that clients with personality disorder are in pain, albeit "hidden pain" (Demmitt & Rueth, 2002).

4. Explore your personal assumptions through an assessment instrument such as Wrightsman's Philosophy of Human Nature Scale (1992), found in Appendix B.

How to Perform Incomplete Assessments

❖
Error #8

❖

Ignoring the Client's "Stage-of-Change" or Commitment Level

Research has identified stage-of-change-related variables as the best predictors of dropout across a growing number of problems, such as heroin addiction, cocaine abuse, alcoholism, domestic violence, obesity, chronic mental illness, and mental health diagnoses.

— N. Prochaska (2001)

As mentioned earlier in this book, a high proportion of patients drop out of therapy unilaterally, and often quite early in treatment. Some studies have found rates as high as fifty percent by the third session. However, not all therapy dropouts are alike. One of the most significant variables that predict dropout rates is the patient's "stage-of-change" factor. Prochaska, cited above, describes six different stages of change, ranging from those clients who see little reason for change (precontemplation stage) to those who are taking active steps to alter their behavioral patterns (action stage). The difference in dropout rates among these groups is striking, with the majority of early terminators coming from the two lowest categories, precontemplation and contemplation. Therefore, it is crucial that therapists know what they are up against before they start formulating "generic" treatment plans.

The next step after assessing a client's state of change is to develop a treatment plan appropriate to that stage. Oftentimes therapists jump the gun by proceeding with treatments that are more appropriate to clients with higher levels of commitment to altering their behavior. For example, when treating substance abuse, implementing reinforcement, stimulus control, and counterconditioning programs are known to be effective with those at the action stage but are likely to fail with the eighty percent of clients who have not reached that stage. However, there is good reason for optimism. As Prochaska indicates, if clients can move just one stage toward a higher commitment to change, the likelihood of a positive outcome is greatly increased.

Thus, the goal for therapists is not always immediate behavior change, as "action-oriented" therapies tend to emphasize. Rather, with "precontemplators" the treatment of choice should utilize consciousness raising and self-reevaluation modalities. We may have been taught that with "at-risk" clients such as pregnant smokers or frequent drug users, "more is better" — meaning a more intense treatment protocol. Nothing could be further from the truth for precontemplators. In fact, treatment that is more intense is often associated with poorer results (Heather, Rollnick, Bell, & Richmond, 1993). We cannot make precontemplators change — what we can do is move them to the contemplation stage.

> A client came to therapy having left his wife for what seemed very good reasons, including her ongoing alcoholism and infidelity. The therapist almost immediately launched into a "postseparation protocol," emphasizing minimum contact between the client and his wife and actions aimed at making his new living quarters more comfortable and home-like for his children's visits. At first the client seemed agreeable to this approach, but more and more he began to discuss whether the marriage warranted "one more try at making it work." Given the extent and history of the marital strife, the therapist did not support the client's goal and repeatedly resumed attempts at having the client "move on." Only when the client reported that he had sneaked home one night to reconnect with his wife did the therapist get the message that the action agenda was premature. The therapist and client then established more appropriate goals related to assessing the marriage's viability. It took

another six months before the client convinced himself that he needed to move on.

Just as therapists can be action-oriented too soon, therapists can also be out of step with clients who are ready, willing, and able to change but just need some guidance, reassurance, and "technical assistance" to do so. Spending too much time on the historical development of the problem can frustrate those who have already reached the commitment stage. Likewise therapists who are nondirective may find that their patients terminate and seek help from more action-oriented therapists.

> One student who had previously been in therapy at a university counseling center complained that all her previous therapist seemed to do was to "rephrase what I said and ask if that was accurate" — when what I really wanted, and even asked for, was some guidance in handling my inconsiderate and messy roommates.

❖ Avoiding the Error

"Stage of change" can be assessed informally during initial sessions by asking the following questions:

1. *Who in your life is most concerned about this problem?*
   If the client is the person most concerned about the difficulty, this can indicate a higher commitment to change. However as is often the case, clients may be coming to therapy at the prodding of another person — their boss, parent, or spouse. In this case, the commitment is lower and indicates that early therapeutic work will need to focus on commitment enhancement.

> Mark, a 39-year-old advertising executive, had been smoking marijuana daily for nearly four years. When asked who cared about this issue the most in his life, he stated, "My girlfriend, she really hates the stuff and has threatened to leave if I don't knock it off." On the one hand, his girlfriend's pressure has certainly worked to get Mark to therapy. On the other hand, other possible benefits of stopping pot smoking need to be discussed as well in order to increase Mark's commitment to change.

2. *What have you done — or thought about doing — about this problem?*

Those clients who have taken action previously are likely to have reached the stage where they recognize that change is only possible through action. Those who have never attempted a change-oriented behavior are still much lower on the commitment scale.

3. *How long has this problem been a concern?*

If a client has been experiencing a problem for a considerable length of time and has finally come to therapy, it can be an indication that the client is ready to take action. On the other hand, it can also indicate that a certain comfort level with the problem has developed. This should be clearly assessed by asking the client what the pros and cons of changing the problem behavior might be.

  a. Recognize that no two clients are alike in terms of their readiness to change or the speed at which they can comfortably proceed. You can neither push the resistant patient nor hold back the action stage patient without harming the therapeutic relationship.

  b. Utilize an informal readiness assessment tool such as the "readiness ruler." This simple yet informative approach involves first clearly specifying an operational behavior the client is interested in changing. Then the therapist holds up a ruler and asks, "Which point on this ruler represents how ready you are at the present time to change your problem behavior?"

  c. Clinicians can also employ a formal "stage-of-change" assessment tool such as the one developed by McConnaughy et al. (1983), which is excerpted in Appendix B.

❖ *Error #9*

Failing to Assess Psychological Reactance

Psychological reactance, is the tendency to resist relinquishing control in interpersonal situations, and generally manifests itself in psychotherapy as behaviors of clients indicative of resistance to change.

— J. Brehm and S. Brehm (1981)

As we have seen, clients come in all sizes and shapes when it comes to commitment to change. Some are ready to tackle the challenge of adopting new ways of acting and thinking — others have essentially been dragged by the hair to their first session.

Similarly, many clients are willing to view the therapist as an "expert" — one who can be trusted to provide needed and valuable guidance — while others view therapy as a battle of wits — a contest in which the client takes up arms against the therapist's power, knowledge, and attempts at interpretation or cognitive and behavioral changes.

The client's receptiveness or resistance to the therapist's formulations is known as *psychological reactance*. This factor must be taken into consideration when determining how directive a therapist should be when implementing a treatment plan. For example, in a group of clients enrolled in a substance abuse program, Karno, Beutler, and Harwood (2002) rated levels of directiveness across therapists who delivered either cognitive-behavioral or family-systems treatment for alcoholism. The results indicated that, regardless of the type of treatment, among high-reactant clients increased therapists' directiveness was associated with increased post-treatment alcohol use. That is, with resistant clients the problem actually got worse with high "directiveness." Conversely, low-reactant clients had a better drinking outcome after following more directive interventions. Similarly, among depressed clients Beutler and Clarkin (1990) found that a supportive and self-directed treatment modality was superior for patients high in reactance as compared with either cognitive-behavioral or focused-expressive therapies. However, for those depressed clients who were low in reactance, the supportive and self-directed treatment was the least effective.

Thus, therapists need to adjust their level of "directiveness" according to the level of the client's resistance. A "one-size-fits-all" approach to treatment planning at its best can be ineffective and at its worst (as in the case of substance abusers) can lead to a worsening of the problem.

> In one case centering on marital conflict, a client "appeared" to be asking for clear direction from the therapist. However, in the midst of making a seemingly helpful recommendation, the client interrupted

to tell the therapist that he was misperceiving the problem and therefore the intervention wouldn't work. In the next session, the client reported that his wife had left him a particularly nasty note. Taking a less directive approach (based on the first week's result), the therapist asked, "What do you think you should do about that?" He replied, "That's why I am here, to get help." The therapist muzzled his impulse to tell the client, "No, you are here to argue" and stated instead that typically brainstorming and collaboration lead to better solutions — and that clients know their situations best. In addition, it was stressed that although the therapist had experience dealing with similar problems and could help generate possible alternatives, the final choice and actual implementation are the client's domain.

❖ Avoiding the Error

1. Be on the alert for signs of reactance in clients, such as interruptions, arguing, off-task comments, and negative responses. Many of these behaviors appear within the first or second session.

2. If the client appears to be high in psychological reactance, develop treatment plans that are less directive and highly collaborative (collaborative approaches are discussed in detail in a later section). If the patient appears to be more cooperative and committed to change, more directive approaches can be undertaken.

3. A formal assessment tool can also be utilized. The Hong Scale of Psychological Reactance (Hong & Page, 1989), found in Appendix B, is a fourteen-item self-report instrument that evaluates the extent to which patients are reluctant to relinquish control in interpersonal situations. Examples of items include "I consider advice to be an intrusion" and "I resist the attempts of others to influence me."

❖
Error #10

Underutilizing Clinical Assessment Instruments

Assessment tools which are used early in therapy to measure the type and intensity of the initial problem and occasionally during the course of treatment can aid in treatment effectiveness, client morale and reducing termination by resistant clients.

— C. D. Booraem, J. V. Flowers, and B. Schwartz (1993)

In spite of the research such as that cited above, clinicians by and large are often skeptical about the value of utilizing assessment tools. For example, one supervising therapist described a case where a postdoctoral intern was not administering a well-known and highly validated assessment tool that was part of an intake protocol at the clinical facility. The trainee stated that she did not "believe in" the assessment tool in that it was not particularly useful and took a lot of time to score — in spite of the fact that the specific instrument had proven its validity and utility in dozens of studies.

There are a number of reasons that contribute to the effectiveness of utilizing assessment instruments:

1. The therapist gains information from a source that allows comparisons to other clients regarding the severity of the problem.

2. Repeating the test at periodic intervals can help demonstrate to the therapist and client whether treatment is being effective.

3. If the results indicate improvement, positive expectations are reinforced. If there is no improvement, the client and therapist can adjust the treatment approach appropriately.

4. Clients tend to see assessment utilization by the therapists as an act of caring, and it enhances client regard for a clinician's expertise.

Although there is a plethora of short and uncomplicated assessment tools available, there are various factors responsible that contribute to their underutilization by clinicians:

1. Many clinicians are unfamiliar with the ever-increasing number of available instruments.

2. Taking the test may infringe on treatment time, and thus clients may feel they are being shortchanged.

3. Scoring and interpreting the test requires considerable time and effort.

4. Some therapists, as in the case cited above, may be skeptical about the value of such instruments (often in spite of significant research to the contrary).

5. Such testing is simply not part of the therapeutic habit.

❖Avoiding the Error

1. Familiarize yourself with the variety of assessment tools available to therapists. Many of these are in the public domain and thus require no financial expenditure. Appendix C at the end of this book lists some of the most useful instruments by clinical category.

2. Recognize that many of these tests require very little time to take or score.

3. Explain to the client the numerous potential benefits of utilizing assessment tools. Do not expect that they will automatically understand why such tools can be helpful to their treatment.

4. Follow up on assessments by providing feedback to the client. Several studies have shown that an open discussion of the results of psychological testing can have beneficial results on therapeutic outcome (Finn & Tonsager, 1992).

Error #11

Failing to Challenge Client "Self-Misdiagnoses"

How, as clinicians, should we go about assessing our clients' assessment of their own problems? In the same way porcupines make love — very cautiously — with a healthy dose of skepticism thrown in as well. From time to time, clients do have a clear sense of the nature of their problem: "I am deathly afraid of public speaking," "I need to be more assertive with my boyfriend," or "I am hooked on pot." However, it is just as common to encounter clients whose self-diagnosis is significantly off target. Such *"mis-diagnoses"* left unevaluated can lead to clinical *"mis-treatment."*

Alex, at 17, had a long history of wreaking havoc at home and at school. His school counselor suspected bipolar disorder and Alex was convinced that he had the worst form of this illness. A psychiatrist was consulted who confirmed the diagnosis of Bipolar Disorder Type II. Lithium was prescribed, but surprisingly the angry outbursts against authority figures increased. After more than a year of this, the parents finally gave up on psychotherapy and medication and sent Alex to live with his aunt in rural Montana. His "unschooled" aunt laid down the law with Alex, who admitted that he had been using quite a bit of cocaine back home. Subsequently, a local psychologist correctly diagnosed Alex as having conduct disorder, and with structure and a drugless regimen he began to make significant progress.

Things get even more complicated when clients have been diagnosed by their spouses, parents, or other armchair therapists.

Brett was referred to the college psychological services because his parents were convinced that he had ADHD. When queried as to why his parents thought this was the case, Brett stated that it was because he often interrupted his parents when they were having a conversation and that from time to time when he was stressed he tended to pace back and forth. Brett had struggled all his life to overcome his stuttering problem and the self-consciousness that accompanied this problem. He was quite upset at his parents labeling of him and was quite relieved to hear that he exhibited none of the criteria that would qualify him for an ADHD diagnosis. His interrupting his parents' conversations had to do with his overlearning of speaking publicly, and was not a sign of impulsivity.

On occasion a discerning therapist can disabuse clients of inaccurate diagnoses.

Mandy, a 36-year-old woman with marital problems, defined her problem quite confidently as "co-dependence." She stated that her husband would not come to therapy because he didn't believe in it but that was understandable because it was her co-dependence that was the source of the marital strife. An initial assessment determined that her husband was not a substance abuser. Thus, the therapist asked her to describe what she meant by being "co-dependent." She stated that she never stood up to her husband, losing any dispute with him because he was more assertive, rational, and quick-witted than she was. She was asked to keep a journal of such disputes, and when she did so, it revealed that the marriage was indeed quite peaceful as long as she went along with everything her husband wanted. Following the journal review process, Mandy acknowledged that perhaps the marital problems were not solely her fault.

❖ Avoiding the Error

1. Be wary of clients who diagnose themselves with the "syndrome *du jour*," that is, those disorders making the rounds of television talk shows and popular magazines. Recent examples include adult ADHD, bipolar disorder, and "repressed memories" of abuse.

2. Be mindful of the tendency of some clients to employ diagnostic labels in order to absolve themselves of the need to take responsibility for their behavior. For example, one college student came to therapy after suddenly developing "social phobia" after she learned she had to take a speech class for college graduation.

❖
Error #12

Failing to Assess for the Possibility of Organic or Medical Conditions

Erica, age 54, stated at her first session that she was about to give up on therapy and life in general. She had been diagnosed with chronic fatigue syndrome, but previous treatment and medication had been ineffective. The clinician did some research on CFS and found that as many as sixty percent of such cases involved serious sleep problems. After sharing this with Erica, she agreed to consult with a sleep specialist who identified and treated her problem successfully.

Although nearly all psychotherapists are trained to be vigilant for medical conditions that could be masking or contributing to a patient's psychological problems, misdiagnosis of such conditions is common. In his book *Finding Care for Depression* (2001), Robert Sealy interviewed over 150 former depressive patients and found that rarely had their treating psychiatrist even considered the possibility that their problems might be the result of medical conditions. Given that psychiatrists are medical doctors, one can only imagine how infrequently nonmedically trained counselors refer clients for medical evaluations.

The scientific literature has identified a number of disorders in which patients were misdiagnosed as having a mental disorder when in reality, an organic disorder (either an organic mental disorder or a medical condition) was the cause of the condition. In the case of 100 patients with depression, for example, a study found that eighteen percent of them were diagnosed as bipolar within two years of their initial diagnosis (Insel & Charney, 2003).

Some of these disorders are listed below along with possible organic or medical problem.

Attention-Deficit/Hyperactivity Disorder	Other neurodevelopmental profiles
Conduct Disorder	Bipolar Disorder type 2
Post Traumatic Stress Disorder	Brain trauma
Panic Disorder	Thyroid Disorder; Setraline or other psychopharmacologically induced akasthisia (inner and often motor motor restlessness).
Depression	Chronic Fatigue Syndrome; Epstein-Barr; Prescription intoxication (e.g., digitalis); Gaucher's Disease (an inherited metabolic disorder in which harmful quantities of fatty substance accumulates in organs)
Schizophrenia	Narcolepsy
Dementia	Deafness
Anorexia Nervosa	Achalasia (an enlargement of the esophagus making swallowing difficult)

❖**Avoiding the Error**

1. Follow all standard-of-care procedures for assessment, including taking a medical and mental history of clients and their family members.

2. During the intake, inquire whether the client has had a recent physical examination. If it has been more than a year, recommend such an exam.

3. Include in your professional library books on this topic such as Elizabeth Klonoff's *Preventing Misdiagnosis of Women* (1997).

❖
Error #13

Ignoring Patient Resources

Milton Erickson was a master when it came to eliciting and building on patient capabilities. In one case he was summoned to the home of a suicidally depressed elderly woman who had recently lost her husband. He noticed the house was full of African Violets and inquired about them. She said that she had raised plants for decades but was no longer interested in them. He also found out that she had been a regular churchgoer. So he asked her if she would be willing to give a wedding day gift of one of her plants each time a couple got married at her church. She reluctantly agreed (it would have been difficult to turn down such a benign request). For several years, she engaged in this pursuit, taking great pride in her new mission, and at her funeral years later, hundreds of grateful "plant-receivers" were in attendance.

The concern for focusing on a client's strengths and not just their deficits may seem baffling at first. After all, don't clients come to therapy wanting to focus on what they are doing incorrectly, not what they are doing well? Perhaps, but they also want to feel capable and confident in their ability to change. Albert Bandura's research on self-efficacy clearly showed that patients who believe in their own inner resources are much more likely to demonstrate positive outcomes in therapy. Thus, a major therapeutic dilemma is created: How can therapy be goal focused, problem centered, skill deficit oriented, and cognitive distortion correcting while at the same time building up the patient's sense of self-efficacy?

To avoid the all-too-common error of focusing exclusively on problem areas and weaknesses, it is essential that we are as methodical in our search for our clients' strengths as we are in searching for the correct clinical diagnosis.

❖Avoiding the Error

1. Early in therapy, identify specific occasions in which the client has been successful, accomplishing tasks similar to the goals being addressed in therapy. For example, if alcohol cessation is the goal, clients should not record just how often they drink but how often the impulse to drink did not lead to consumption (Horvath, 2003). In another case, a client who complained that no matter how hard she tried she never mastered difficult tasks was reminded of her success in self-defense training, which she initially saw as "too challenging."

2. Acknowledge and celebrate within the therapy session any accomplishments in the direction of the therapeutic goal. Many clients, for example, who do not follow up on their homework assignments either complete some segment of it or perhaps modify the assignment in a way that allows for completion.

> Alice, who had committed to leaving a long-term abusive relationship, did not succeed in researching available shelters in her area. She was prepared for her therapist's disappointment when she stated, "I didn't do anything this week that we talked about." Instead of dwelling on the failure, the discussion revealed that she had talked to her father for the very first time about her situation. Facing her father's disapproval was actually a much bigger success than the original assignment, and this "success" then became her reference point for recognizing her ability to tackle further challenges.

How to Ignore Science

There is a consensus that counselors and psychotherapists are largely indifferent to, or suspicious about, research findings.

— D. Williams and J. Irving (1999)

Quantitative Research Science is seen as antithetical to the values of person-centered and dynamic counseling — and worse might well be doing a sort of violence to the values on which humanistic therapeutic philosophy is based.

— R. House (1997)

In a recent survey of mental health clinicians, the practice of keeping up with current clinical research was rated as the *lowest* of professional priorities (Watkins & Schneider, 1991). What is surprising is that this anti-science, anti-research sentiment was found even in graduates of programs where a focus on research was a central component of their training.

The results of this widespread indifference toward research is that year after year therapists undertake new, unproven, and scientifically unsound treatments for individuals, couples, and children. From "rebirthing" to "recovered memories," those working in the mental health field seem as susceptible to the latest therapeutic trends and fads as the general public is to new diet crazes. One can understand how the average person might be hoodwinked into trying to lose weight by eating only grapefruit. However, we should expect more from clinicians who are trained to critically assess the claims of those promoting breakthroughs in the treatment of mental disorders. There are a number of reasons for this indifference to "science."

❖ *Error #14*

Disregarding the Data

Which of the following conditions require highly specific treatments of choice if patients are to be helped: obsessive compulsive disorder, eating disorders, post-traumatic stress disorder, sexual disorders, phobias, substance abuse.

Forgive us for the trick question. The answer, of course, is all of the above. Lambert (1992) found that nearly eighty-five percent of patients with mild to moderate levels of distress recovered fairly well from virtually any credible therapeutic approach. However, for many conditions, such as those listed above, it is necessary to employ well-researched treatment protocols that have proven superior to other forms of therapy. However, many clinicians simply disregard the data and instead continue to employ unproven or even disproved methodologies.

> At a continuing education seminar on emerging treatment models, the presenter was discussing various techniques used in the treatment of phobias such as desensitization and imagery. One member of the audience remarked that these "behavioral approaches" missed the underlying roots of the problem and other symptoms would soon pop up unless these issues were resolved first.

Such objections were raised decades ago — and proven baseless — and yet still linger in the hearts and souls of many clinicians. Because some therapists disregard scientifically validated treatment protocols, clients continue to undergo questionable treatment protocols such as Jungian dream analysis to treat social phobia, focusing on "abandonment issues" for post-traumatic stress disorder, or doing "inner-child work" with substance abusers.

❖ *Error #15*

Attending to the Messenger Not the Message

Unfortunately, clinicians are all too human when it comes to being influenced by the "charisma" factor. Without naming names, our field has produced innumerable "snake charmers" whose personal magnetism enabled them to seduce the masses, including those who should have known better. From primal screaming to nude encounter groups, clinicians flocked to the feet of these self-proclaimed gurus, with sometimes disastrous results. John Flowers recounts such an experience:

> Early in my clinical training, my professors recommended that I attend a "marathon" encounter-type group — this was in the "touchy feely" days and such experiences were seen as a way to broaden one's training. The leader was quite well known and I thought it was a valuable opportunity to sit at the feet of a psychology celebrity, who we shall call Dr. Renowned. After a number of hours of group work (we were all pretty exhausted by then), a rather shy female became the group's focus, and her "shyness" became the identified problem. As the group kept pressuring her for more and more personal disclosures, a couple of us novices began to defend her obvious wish to discontinue the interrogation. Instead of granting this respite, the group now turned its attack on us. The two of us weathered the attack fairly well, only minor bruises; however, the young woman began to decompensate in the group. Finally, and against the renowned doctor's advice, we called for an ambulance. The "victim" was taken to a hospital, evaluated, and put on a seventy-two-hour hold.

❖ Avoiding the Error

1. Recognize that experts like the rest of us may have blind spots where ego overtakes knowledge.

2. Apply the same standards of critical thinking regardless of a person's status or prior accomplishments.

3. Remember, charisma is seductive, but as this case demonstrates it is no substitute for substance.

Error #16

Achieving Theoretical Rigor Mortis

Therapists, like all human beings, find security in establishing a system of beliefs. However, many practitioners hold an almost religious allegiance to their theoretical positions. Such inflexibility does not allow for conflicting data to be rationally evaluated. It is very easy to become so attached to one's school of therapy that any facts that do not fit the school are ignored or "bent" into the belief system. Thus, research may be seen as the enemy to these emotionally held principles.

> Dr. Assertion ran groups and came to the belief that assertion was the cure for most if not all interpersonal problems. In one group, a young teenage boy, whose father was an alcoholic, was coached to be assertive when his father mistreated his mother and him. As the result of "standing up for himself," the boy ended up in the hospital — fortunately with no permanent damage — and the father in jail.

Again, more attention to the research on assertion would have raised a red flag about the conditions under which assertion is not only ineffective, but even dangerous.

❖ Avoiding the Error

1. Develop treatment plans that are consistent with the current research that is available on the disorder. Familiarize yourself with the respected journals that focus on the clinical application of research. Many of these journals are found in the bibliography at the end of this book.

2. Review "breakthrough" treatments that are touted on television shows (e.g., *Dr. Phil* and *Oprah*) or newspapers with a skeptic's eye until you have seen a published study or three in a reputable journal.

3. Remain open to new information that challenges your currently held clinical beliefs. Theoretical approaches are not "religious dogma"; to question the tenets of an approach when new evidence is presented is, therefore, not blasphemy.

An example of this involves research that we conducted at the height of the "co-dependency is everywhere" epoch. At that time not only were many therapists sold on the validity of the concept, there was a serious movement to make this into another diagnosis within the *Diagnostic and Statistical Manual.*

The research we undertook demonstrated that clients who were diagnosed by their therapists or themselves as co-dependent, or who tested high on the traits of the syndrome on assessment instruments, were more adequately diagnosed by the criteria for personality disorders. Moreover, the present diagnostic system gave more specific information and did not lump all these clients into a one-size-fits-all category.

This is not to say that co-dependency is not a useful concept, but rather that it is an "umbrella term" like *anxiety* or *depression* that must be more finely assessed to be helpful in generating treatment plans. The first time these data were presented, the authors were accused of therapeutic "heresy."

How to Avoid Collaboration with the Client

Collaboration empowers clients by giving them a say in their own therapeutic process — and it fosters self-efficacy.

— C. Feltham and I. Horton (2000)

When shopping for real estate, experts tell you that the value of homes is based on three principles: location, location, location. Similarly, when it comes to setting treatment goals and expectations for therapy, the key is collaboration, collaboration, collaboration.

Collaboration is a process in which therapist and patient work together as partners throughout the therapeutic process. In the collaborative role the therapist can be viewed as the senior partner, taking the lead in most matters while eliciting and responding to feedback from his or her "associate."

Error #17

Setting Goals Unilaterally

June had been in an abusive marriage for over fifteen years. Recently, things had worsened as her husband's drinking had increased. He would come home extremely late on the weekends thoroughly intoxicated and demand extended periods of sexual activity. He would then stumble around, urinating "like a cat" in various living areas. The client asked the therapist if her husband was an alcoholic and what kind of treatment programs might be appropriate. In this case, the therapist responded in the "traditional" manner, focusing on the "battered-wives treatment protocol," that is, an escape plan was formulated and a referral was made to a battered-women's support group and shelter. In spite of his best efforts, the therapist was quite disappointed to learn that the patient did not schedule a follow-up appointment.

In this case, the therapist followed the recommended "standard of care" and yet the client did not follow up on these recommendations and — worse yet — terminated therapy. What went wrong? Most likely, a lack of collaboration in formulating treatment goals. In this case the therapist unilaterally decided on the therapeutic agenda, an agenda that did not match the client's. Nowhere in this session did the client ask the therapist whether she should consider leaving her husband. Indeed, a review of the transcript shows that the client was still convinced that her husband might "see the light," alter his behavior, and be the husband that she wished for. Of course the therapist and anyone else hearing about the case could clearly see that after fifteen years, the likelihood of significant change was low, but that doesn't mean that the client was of like mind.

Thus, while therapists must certainly provide appropriate information and resources to abused individuals, we must also address the client's stated concerns. In a collaborative approach, therapist and client are on the same page. In order to arrive at that page, the therapist facilitates a discussion of possible treatment goals and then helps the client to prioritize these goals and choose which ones to focus on initially.

❖ Avoiding the Error

1. Explain the difference between collaborative and noncollaborative approaches to the client. Emphasize the importance of the client's input, feedback, and agreement on all aspects of goal setting and treatment.

2. Pay as much attention to what clients are *not* saying as to what they *are* saying. For example, in the case cited above the client's stated concern was to find out what kind of treatment options were available for her husband. One thing she never mentioned was whether she should leave this relationship. Of course as

the therapeutic alliance develops, this option could certainly be brought up by the therapist.

3. Use an "open-ended" questioning approach, not a "lecturing" or didactic approach. Gerald Monk, in his book *Narrative Therapy in Practice* (1997), describes the importance of using open-ended questions to achieve three significant therapeutic purposes. Some examples include

  a. *to clarify and prioritize goals:*
  What kind of difficulties is this problem causing you now?
  What kind of difficulties might it cause you in the future?
  What goals might a person (not necessarily you) have in this situation?
  Which goals fit you?
  Which goals do not?

  b. *to increase personal efficacy:*
  When have you been able to "shake off" or free yourself from this problem?
  Have you observed how other people have dealt with similar situations successfully?
  In your fantasies, how have you tackled the problem successfully?

  c. *to increase commitment to change:*
  If you change, how will your life be better?
  How will your life be worse if things do not change?
  Where can you go to get support for your attempts to change?

❖ *Error #18*

Failing to Develop Collaborative Goals in Early Sessions

When a solid goal and treatment consensus is built early in therapy, treatment outcomes measured months later are more likely to be positive. This research found reductions in depressive symptoms six months after the inception of treatment, when patients experienced goals consensus following the SECOND session.

— J. Dormaar, C. Dijkman, and M. de Vries (1989)

It is important not only to develop a consensus on treatment goals, it is important to do so as early as possible in the therapeutic process. Often therapists look at early sessions as a "getting to know you" period, leaving the real work of therapy for later sessions, spending the bulk of the time filling out forms, reviewing office policies, and taking a detailed clinical history. Certainly some attention should be paid to these matters, but the first and second session should also set the stage for the achievement of goal consensus. When this occurs, client expectations for success are greatly increased, and client expectations are significant predictors of positive outcomes.

Imagine going to the family physician with various symptoms, and following the examination the doctor simply schedules a follow-up appointment without providing some sense of what the problem might be and what kind of treatments would be appropriate. The only goal you would have upon leaving the office would be that of seeking a referral for a new family doctor. The situation is no different for clients seeking help with psychological problems.

> One client reported that her previous therapist (emphasis on *previous*) was still assessing the problem after two full sessions. This was a case in which she was procrastinating on a term paper that was due "any minute," wondering how to tell her parents that she was homosexual, and overly concerned about diet and eating issues.

In this case it seems as if there were plenty of treatment goals to select from. However, the former therapist seemed to be suffering from "paralysis from analysis" — or assessment in this case.

❖Avoiding the Error

1. Leave time at the end of the first session to clarify the client's concerns and to rephrase them as possible treatment goals. For example, in the case of the "procrastinating student," a therapist could state, "It seems there are a number of areas that are causing you distress — completing a term paper, eating issues, and discussing your sexual orientation with your

parents. Do you have a sense of which one of these would be most important to focus on initially?"

2. Praise clients when they add to a solution. An enthusiastic "That's better than what I had in mind," or "that's a good addition" helps to increase commitment.

3. Expand your definition of what it means to be a psychotherapist to include aspects of consulting, coaching, and leadership.

4. Recognize that goal setting is not restricted to the reduction of problems such as depression, anxiety, or substance abuse but can and should include attention to positive behaviors that can be increased. Such goals can involve coping skills, relapse prevention, and expansion of those aspects of the client's life that are life enhancing.

5. Do not assume that what appears to be the "obvious goal" is what the client has in mind as most significant.

❖ *Error #19*

Failing to Include the Client in Setting Session Agendas

A collaborative relationship does not begin and end with the determination of goals and a course of action. Asking clients at the beginning of each session what they would like to focus or work on is an invitation to re-engage them in active therapy. Also, in this way, treatment goals are continually updated and modified as therapy progresses. Such updating has been found to improve client satisfaction, reduce distress, and increase expectations of success. For example, Hoyt, Xenakis, and Marmar (1983) found that clients were more likely to rate sessions as "good therapy hours" when treatment goals and approaches to problem solving were discussed.

❖Avoiding the Error

1. Begin each session with goal setting to avoid the tendency to let the goal simply "emerge" as an unspoken, tacit agreement.

Always state the goal, no matter how obvious it seems, and check to see if there is agreement.

2. Before questioning the client on the specific goal, write down what you as a therapist presently believe the goal is or should be.

3. Recognize that for some clients, one of the main goals can be to develop a goal. Such clients often formulate ambiguous, overly complex goals or shift their focus from one issue to another throughout the session. With such clients, a "brainstorming" protocol can be employed, in which ideas are tossed out by both therapist and client, generating a list that can then be prioritized.

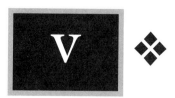

How to Ruin the Therapist-Client Relationship

It is imperative that clinicians remember that decades of research consistently demonstrate that relationship factors correlate more highly with client outcome than do specialized treatment techniques.

— L. Castenguay, M. Goldfried, S. Wiser,
P. Raue, and A. Hayes (1996)

In many studies, what therapists say and do in the therapy hour that promotes a good working alliance has proven to be the most important contributor to change and positive treatment outcome.

— E. Teyber and F. McClure (2000)

To borrow a phrase from renowned football coach Vince Lombardi: The therapeutic alliance isn't everything in psychotherapy — it's the only thing. To be more precise, no other single factor affects therapy outcomes more than the quality of the client-therapist relationship. Although it is difficult to ascertain exact percentages of therapeutic effect, one study did attempt to do just that. After reviewing over 100 outcome studies, Lambert and Barley (2001) derived an estimate of the relative contribution of the myriad factors that have been studied in outcome research. Surprisingly, the specific techniques employed by therapists (cognitive, psychodynamic, etc.) accounted for only thirty percent of therapeutic outcome. However, the quality of the client-therapist relationship predicted results forty percent of the time. Factors influencing this relationship include credibility, trustworthiness, and the expertness of the clinician. Of course, the therapeutic relationship by itself should not be considered an "intervention." Rather as Edward Bordin, a pioneer in the development of the working alliance, put it, the client-therapist bond "...is a vehicle that enables and facilitates the specific counseling techniques..." employed by the clinician (1980).

Error #20

Emphasizing Technique over Relationship Building

Sometimes I'm not careful enough to build a relationship with the client before pointing out that he or she may have made some bad choices.

— W. Glasser (2003)

An intern related to her ever-patient supervisor that she had been learning about the use of "paradoxical intention" in her advanced counseling class. She was hoping to try out this dramatic new technique with one of her clients and did so with a patient during their very first session. The patient had returned to school after a recent divorce and complained of being totally overwhelmed. She couldn't get herself to do any homework and was no longer the paragon of organization she used to be — failing to do even the simplest of chores like laundry or dishes. The intervention the intern tried was to "join the symptom" and prescribe the homework assignment to do "absolutely no work at all this week" and report back at the next session how this went. Unfortunately, there was no next session — the client requested a different therapist from the director of the clinic.

The lesson here is one that is all too commonly missed: The therapeutic relationship trumps technique. It is all well and good to have available a wide variety of techniques, interventions, and therapeutic tools, but interviews with clients repeatedly show that without a foundation of a solid working alliance, there is little chance that even the most brilliant intervention will be implemented. This is particularly true when utilizing "high-risk" techniques such as those based on paradoxical intention — which require a high degree of client trust.

In this case, the assessment of the client's problem was accurate and the intervention might at some later date have proven effective — if the client had stuck around long enough to find out. The tendency to rush into the therapist tool kit and resolve the problem quickly is of course exacerbated by the current emphasis on brief or time-limited therapy. Suffice it to say, the "bottom line orientation" ("time is money") is not always in the patient's best interests.

❖ Avoiding the Error

In early sessions, emphasize relationship building by focusing on the following factors associated with therapeutic effectiveness:

1. Enhance your credibility by describing your experience with other cases similar to the client's in which there was a successful outcome.

2. Emphasize genuineness by not behaving in an overly formal manner. One surveyed client described why she felt comfortable with her therapist by stating, "I appreciated the fact that he was so natural." Remember, a clinician can be "the expert" without losing his or her humanity.

3. Convey positive regard by indicating your interest in working together with the client to resolve the presenting issues.

4. Before introducing any interventions, particularly those of a complex or unusual nature, reflect on the following:
   - ❖ Do I have a thorough enough grasp of the history and nature of the problem?
   - ❖ Do I know this client well enough to determine the appropriateness of this intervention?
   - ❖ Does the client know and trust me sufficiently to have confidence in my therapeutic skills?

Even though you may have all of your licenses, credentials, and degrees prominently and tastefully displayed on your office walls, it takes time and relationship building to gain the confidence of most clients.

❖ *Error #21*

Failing to Communicate Sufficient Empathy and Other Signs of Support

Patients who felt that their therapy was successful described their therapist as "warm, attentive, interested, understanding, and respectful."

— H. Strupp, R. Fox, and K. Lessler (1969)

What graduate student hasn't memorized and practiced repeatedly Carl Rogers's three imperatives: unconditional positive regard, therapist congruence, and empathic understanding? And yet many clients terminate therapy because they feel that their therapists lack one or more of these qualities. In fact, in a study of therapists who sought out their own personal therapy, over thirty percent reported that they felt that their therapists did not care about them, that empathy was lacking (Curtis, Field, Knaan-Kostman, & Mannis, 2004). Of Rogers's therapeutic triad, empathy has been the most researched. Dozens of studies have identified numerous benefits resulting from therapist empathy. These include increased client satisfaction, enhanced feelings of safety, and greater retention in therapy. And that's just the beginning. Empathy has been found to help clients think more productively (Sachse, 1990); it facilitates emotional reprocessing (Greenberg & Paivio, 1997); and finally it helps therapists choose interventions compatible with the client's frame of reference. Empathy has been emphasized as a vital component of therapy by clinicians from a wide variety of therapeutic orientations, including Adlerian, behavioral, cognitive, and rational emotive. Yet this fundamental quality is often found to be lacking in even the most experienced therapist.

> A patient complained to her renowned therapist that she was offended by his rather formal and distant attitude when she discussed her difficulty coping with her husband's terminal illness. A rather outspoken woman, she stated that he seemed unfeeling and "did not bring his own self into the sessions." The therapist "brooded about this...and concluded that she was correct." He then admitted his error to her at the next session and asked for help in the future to

remind him when he was off course. This admission helped to repair the damaged relationship so that effective therapy could then take place (Yalom, 1997).

Clearly, clients don't feel this lack of empathy because the majority of therapists don't really feel warmly toward their clients. After all, most people who go into the mental health field are genuinely caring and supportive individuals. What the research does suggest, however, is a disconnect between the level of empathy therapists think they are communicating and what clients are receiving.

❖ Avoiding the Error

1. Begin every session by making eye contact when greeting the patient. This is particularly necessary "late in the day" when you may be running out of steam. A handshake and greeting can communicate much more to the client than the typical "How did your week go?"

2. From the beginning of therapy, engage clients as respected equals who you care about understanding. As one master therapist put it, "Because I have heard more clients come in saying that they felt hurt or disrespected if people were too curt with them — like they're not interested. . . . I always ask them early on, 'Do you feel understood and respected?'" (Jennings, Sovereign, & Bottorff, 2005).

3. Be mindful of your feelings toward your client. Ask yourself, "Do I empathize with this client and his or her problem?" Do not start by asking the question, "Am I communicating empathy?" — ask if you feel it. If the answer is "I don't really feel this enough," one of the following two assessments will usually help.
   a. Do I need to hear more of what the client is feeling about this to connect?
   b. Do I need to imagine how I would feel in this situation to connect?

Error #22

Believing That Empathy and Unconditional Positive Regard Means Liking Your Patient

At a recent continuing education seminar on domestic violence, the lecturer asked the thirty or so participants whether they would prefer to work with perpetrators or victims. A large majority chose victims as preferable clients. The presenter was one of the few who found the work with perpetrators challenging and fulfilling. Others thought that it would be nearly impossible to have positive regard for people who are so unlikable. After all, these are potentially dangerous people who abuse their power in relationships to control, demean, and harm those they are supposed to care for.

The misconception here is that having positive regard for someone equates to liking the person. It would be asking the impossible to expect ourselves to feel abundant warmth for those whose actions make them highly unappealing, such as those who commit domestic violence. However, as Carl Rogers has indicated, "Unconditional positive regard involves a feeling of acceptance for the client's expression of negative, 'bad', painful, fearful, defensive, abnormal feelings as for his expression of 'good', positive, mature, confident, social feelings" (1955).

Thus, the goal is not to like people who engage in deplorable behavior, but rather to accept people as they are at present — and to believe that they are "helpable." And the fact is, many are quite "helpable." For domestic violence perpetrators, for example, recent statistics show that those who complete a ten-week psychoeducational program are much less likely to repeat offend (Palmer et al., 1992).

What is required of therapists who work with such cases is to explore that person's background so that the behavior is seen in its full context — not so it can be justified but as a means to recognize the source and power of their attitudes and impulsivity.

Therapist Mark Freeman relates a dramatic case that illustrates the need to look beyond the horrific actions a person may commit. The case involved a father who had been plotting to kill his wife and children and then himself. The plans were discovered and he was immediately jailed, awaiting long-term hospitalization. For weeks, nurses and therapists kept their distance, due to a combination of fear and abhorrence for the man.

This continued until it became known that he had been diagnosed with terminal colon cancer and was not expected to live more than six months. When his previously distant therapist was made aware of this, he began to engage with his client and it was further revealed that he had always been a loving and involved husband and father, but that along with his cancer he had significant financial stressors as well. His businesses were going under and he could only foresee great suffering for his family in the future. Not only would they have to deal with his death, but he envisioned a life of destitution for them.

His convoluted reasoning led him to believe that all would be better off dead. This revelation led the therapist to change his view of the client, allowing him to work productively to reunite the family and plan productively for the challenges ahead (Freeman & Hayes, 2002).

❖ Avoiding the Error

1. "Try to connect with the person behind the repulsive or repugnant behavior or attitude" (Wilkins, 2000). To connect with such individuals means first recognizing that their acts are not the totality of who they are; it means seeking information about the person's strengths, successes, and goals.

2. Recognize that it is from the client's strengths, not weaknesses, that change will come. If perpetrators sense you like some part of them, but not what they did, that you have faith that they can change and will like them even more when they do, the likelihood of a strong therapeutic alliance is increased dramatically.

3. Separate the emotion that led your clients to the aberrant act from the act they committed that elicits your negative emotions. Imagine the emotion leading to a different action, a different object, or a different place. In other words, determine what

you want them to do with the feeling and then actually imagine in your mind's eye the client engaging in the appropriate behavior. For example, imagine a client who has been involved in domestic violence engaging in prosocial problem solving when feeling angry.

4. Realize that if you help modify a perpetrator's behavior, you may be preventing harm to many potential victims.

5. Be careful of counter-contagion. Just as the therapist must resist the emotional contagion of the client who naturally elicits our empathy, the mental health professional must also resist the reactive contagion elicited when the client naturally elicits fear, anger, or, worst of all, disgust.

❖ *Error #23*

Failing to Elicit Client Feedback on the Alliance

In follow-up studies of "unilateral terminators" most therapists only became aware of their client's dissatisfaction after their termination. In fact, in a further study only seventeen to thirty percent of therapists (depending on level of experience) could identify the specific areas of dissatisfaction which their UT clients reported.

— B. Reis and L. Brown (1999)

Unfortunately, most clients do not directly convey the negative feelings they may have toward their therapists or the treatment process. Many clients are somewhat passive and eager to please and may see voicing their dissatisfactions as highly confrontational. Thus, therapists must convey to their clients that they expect and welcome feedback. This encouragement begins in the initial session, and client feedback should be a regular component of the therapeutic agenda. Even though eliciting feedback can be helpful, therapists can be highly resistant to the idea, perhaps fearing that they will receive answers they would rather not hear.

A second-year trainee complained in his group supervision class that he was making very little progress with a difficult case. When asked by a group member to describe the quality of the therapeutic relationship, the trainee stated that he regularly assessed therapist-client rapport and that it seemed to be quite positive. It was decided that reviewing a videotape of a session with this client would be helpful. When reviewing the tape, it was noted that the client seemed quite distant and his answers were brief, and there was so much silence we checked the VCR to see if the sound was on. At no point did the therapist inquire about the client's seeming reluctance to talk and whether he had an issue or concern about therapy or the therapist. When this was pointed out to the trainee, he was adamant in stating that he had in fact inquired about the relationship. We rewound the entire tape and asked the trainee to stop the tape following an "alliance"-related question. He did so after his very first question which was, "So, how did your week go?"

Needless to say, "How did your week go?" is an appropriate session opener but does not easily lead to an exploration of the therapist-client relationship.

❖ Avoiding the Error

1. Ask clients direct questions, such as "Was there anything about today's session that was helpful or unhelpful." Such questions make it crystal clear that therapy is a shared enterprise — and an ongoing one. It sends the message that the therapist is not all knowing — and that the client's insights, feedback, and questions are accepted and appreciated.

2. At the beginning of sessions, ask clients whether they have thought any more about the last session? If the answer is yes (and it will be ever more so if you ask regularly), follow up by exploring what was most helpful and whether clients feel that anything was left unfinished?

3. Utilize a formal therapeutic alliance assessment tool. A multitude of such instruments have been developed to provide clinicians with a snapshot of the client's perspective on the quality of the therapeutic alliance. The following three instruments are readily available and are quite easy to score.

The Counselor Satisfaction Questionnaire — Short Form

The majority of clients who drop out of therapy do so by the fourth session. Thus it is imperative that therapists receive accurate feedback from their clients as early as possible. The CSQ-S (Stokes & Lauterschlager, 1978) provides such feedback quickly and conveniently. It consists of the following four questions, which are rated using a four-point Likert-type scale (questions can be adapted to specific clinical settings).

1. In an overall, general sense, how satisfied were you with your first session?

2. To what extent did the interview address your immediate concerns?

3. If you were to seek help again would you return for counseling?

4. Are these first sessions going in the direction you wish?

The Counselor Rating Form — Short

The CRF-S (Corrigan & Schmidt, 1983) allows therapists to receive feedback on their clinical strengths and weaknesses. It consists of a list of thirty-six statements that describe a variety of clinical behaviors. The items are grouped into three subscales that measure three skill areas: therapist expertness, trustworthiness, and attractiveness. Each of these areas has been shown to predict the depth of the client-therapist bond, which in turn predicts therapeutic outcome.

The Working Alliance Inventory

The WAI, developed in 1989 by Adam Horvath and Leslie Greenberg, built on Bordin's three dimensions of counseling effectiveness: tasks, goals, and bonds. "Task"-focused questions investigate the substance of the counseling process, e.g., "I find what I am doing in therapy confusing." The "goals" component of the inventory concerns therapy outcomes, e.g., "I know what to expect as a result of my therapy." "Bonds" refers to the emotional connection between client and therapist, e.g., "I believe my therapist is genuinely concerned for my welfare." The complete WAI is included in Appendix B.

❖ *Error #24*

Ignoring the Client's Verbal and Nonverbal Feedback

Therapists need to be sensitive to the risk that their own estimate of the status of the relationship, particularly in the opening phases of therapeutic work, can be at odds with the client's.

— A. O. Horvath and B. D. Symonds (1991)

Even with encouragement, many clients may still feel uncomfortable expressing their concerns about the process and/or progress of therapy. Thus, therapists may go happily along their way thinking that all is fine between client and clinician, when in fact it is not.

An interesting study by Barrett-Lennard (1981) addresses this issue. His research investigated the following question: "Whose ratings of therapist empathy predicted therapeutic outcome best — the client's, a trained observer's, or the therapist's?" The surprising answer is that only the client's perception of the therapist's level of empathy was a significant predictor of therapeutic outcome. In other words, clinicians may feel warmly toward their client and may even think that they are exuding that warmth, whereas the client may view the therapist as lukewarm or even slightly chilled.

❖ Avoiding the Error

In order to accurately read a client's comfort level with the process and progress of therapy, clinicians needs to be alert for subtle "alliance" indicators by assessing the following:

1. Is the client making less eye contact than previously during sessions? A decrease in eye contact indicates a changed internal state in the client, which can indicate decreased trust of the therapist or an emotion or experience the client does not feel comfortable sharing.

2. Is the client disclosing less about personal matters and instead relating tangential or less therapeutically relevant material?

3. Are the greetings at the beginning of the session less cordial than at earlier times?

❖ *Error #25*

❖

Responding Defensively to Negative Client Feedback

In a study of client feedback, Castenguay et al. (1996) found that a large number of clinicians ignored, minimized, or counterattacked when clients voiced their concerns. For example, many psychodynamic therapists viewed their client's dissatisfaction as "resistance." They then proceeded to explore the basis for this resistance, nicely shifting any blame away from themselves. In the same study, cognitive therapists were discovered to often view the client's comments as cognitive distortions related to unrealistic expectations about therapy and thus they tried to restructure their "irrational" thoughts. As for the clients in the study, they often verbally agreed with their therapists that their criticism was unwarranted. However, there's the rub; following their admission of culpability, many did not return for further counseling. The battle won, the war lost.

We have been suggesting that to nurture the therapeutic relationship and to enhance therapeutic progress, it is necessary to elicit any negative feedback the client may have. However, it is one thing to invite feedback, it is quite another to respond to this feedback in a productive and nondefensive matter. At the heart of the matter is that however hard therapists try to be helpful, supportive, and attentive, inevitably there will be times when clients feel insulted, neglected, misunderstood, or disappointed in their therapeutic progress.

> A client who was being treated for stress and health-related problems began to appear less involved in the treatment process — coming late to sessions, appearing apathetic, and not completing out-of-session activities. The therapist brought up the matter by stating, "It feels like I am doing something wrong with you. Am I?" The client was very sensitive in replying. "You know," she began, "you really know your stuff about stress and health. It's just that I feel like you've done this a whole lot before — but, well, you don't know me very well." The therapist was taken aback but apologized and asked the client to share more about herself that would be important for him to know — and by so doing discovered she had significant fears that no matter what

she attempted at this point, her health problems were too severe to be overcome. She had essentially resigned herself to dying.

Here was a case where the therapist was being his usual expert self in the process of assessment and treatment planning. What had been left out was letting the patient tell her own story in her own time. What saved the day was the therapist's asking for input about why therapy wasn't proceeding well and then taking stock of the situation and taking corrective actions, which involved dealing with her sense of hopelessness — a fundamental issue that needed to be resolved before moving on to specific "therapeutic interventions."

❖Avoiding the Error

When dealing with negative feedback from clients, it is important to keep the following in mind:

1. The fact that clients feel safe enough with you to voice their concerns indicates that there is trust in the therapeutic relationship.

2. Clients respect therapists who can admit their own fallibility.

3. You can use the possible "rupture" in the relationship as a means to show that relationships can withstand difficulties when people are honest and willing to problem solve. One therapist described the process this way: "What I would say to clients is that a therapy relationship is like all other relationships. Even though sometimes we wouldn't want it to be, it is, and how we repair the rupture in our relationship can also help with ruptures occurring in other relationships. This could be a place where that could happen and serve as a model for that in other experiences" (Sullivan, Skovhold, & Jennings, 2005).

How to Set Improper Therapist-Client Boundaries

...Counselors must operate in boundary terms in a manner that enables them to move across the counselor client interpersonal line — for identification purposes — but at the same time they must remain firmly anchored within their own boundary space — for objectivity purposes.

— B. Hermansson (1997)

Sounds easy enough — we have heard it a thousand times throughout our training: "Maintain appropriate boundaries." But ask ten therapists what their definition of *boundaries* is and you are likely to get twelve answers. The most common notion of boundary "mistakes" involves inappropriate romantic or sexual behavior. However, boundary errors can involve a wide variety of complex behaviors. So let us begin this discussion with an attempt at definitions. A good starting place is the description provided by Katherine (1991) in which a boundary is defined as a "limit or edge that defines us as separate from others...which brings order to our lives and gives us a clearer sense of ourselves and our relationship with others." Taking it one step further, Hermansson (1997) introduces the concepts of fusion and individuation. Fusion is a "blurring of the boundaries between patient and therapist — a state of role confusion." At the other extreme are therapists who remain coolly detached from their patients, maintaining boundaries that are too rigid and inflexible.

❖ *Error #26*

Overidentifying with the Patient

When therapists "fuse" or overidentify with their patients, they go well beyond expressing empathy; they not only put themselves in their patients' shoes, they lose themselves in the process. The result is a significant lack of objectivity. Interestingly, therapists with high fusion tendencies report being highly stressed about their patients' well-being and also have significant doubts about their own professional abilities (Hellman, Morrison, & Abramowitz, 1987).

Therapists who work with victims of abuse trauma are especially prone to overidentification. In such cases therapists often attempt to "rescue" their patients, offering help and availability far beyond what is therapeutically appropriate. Some therapists with inordinate rescue fantasies take on increasing numbers of patients with the most severe difficulties. Their work becomes a mission — one that, unfortunately, often leads to therapist burnout.

In spite of the therapist's good intentions, the message that often comes across to these clients is "Your suffering is of such a magnitude that it will take enormous resources and personal support from me for you to recover." This opens the door for the patient (and therapist) to breach appropriate boundaries and to become excessively dependent on one another.

However, overidentification does not always result from work with traditional trauma cases. In one case a woman wished for help coping with an "empty marriage in which the husband was very neglectful and absorbed in his career and children." She wanted to remain in the marriage until such a time as the children left for college. The intern handling this case began to absorb the client's increasing loneliness and sense of hopelessness at being unable to change the situation in any significant way. After much discussion with her supervisor, the intern decided it would be useful for her to receive some therapy regarding the basis for her "overidentification" problem, and the client's case was taken over by the supervisor.

❖**Avoiding the Error**

1. Recognize that working effectively with patients does not mean that you "feel their pain." It means that you express your understanding of the depth of pain that the client is feeling. For example, a client reveals with great anguish that a long-term relationship has ended. Certainly a caring therapist recognizes the distress the patient is expressing with statements such as, "I am truly sorry for your loss, I know how much this relationship meant to you." However, it is important to separate yourself from the patient's loss, that is, it not helpful to join with the grieving as if both of you have lost a relationship.

2. Consider that working with highly disturbed patients and those who have been victims of trauma requires special attention not only to the patient's well-being but to the therapist's as well.

3. Every effort must be made to maintain one's emotional equilibrium when clients recount instances of abuse and trauma. Appropriate steps of therapist self-care must be taken, and efforts to build a practice around trauma victims must be evaluated seriously.

4. Be self-reflective regarding the amount of the client's pain you are absorbing and how this is affecting your effectiveness and emotional well-being. Ask yourself if your own boundaries are being taxed by what you are feeling and whether your emotions are too high for you to be therapeutically effective.

❖ *Error #27*

Allowing Inappropriate Levels of Physical Intimacy

Whatever houses I may visit, I will come for the benefit of the sick, remaining free of all intentional injustice... and in particular of sexual relations with both female and male persons, be they free or slaves.

— *The Hippocratic Oath* (c. 400 BC)

The clearest example of overstepping boundaries involves the fusion of the professional and the romantic. In spite of Hippocrates's proclamation over 2,500 years ago, it was not until recently that severe injunctions against romantic involvement with therapy patients were enacted. Such behavior is now viewed as unethical, intrusive, and exploitative — a violation of the trust that must be inherent in the therapeutic endeavor. It is also recognized that this is true regardless of who initiates the sexual advances. Nonetheless, ten to twenty percent of therapists (depending on the study) admit to having sexual contact with their patients. And this violation is not restricted to unseasoned therapists. In a survey of "senior" psychologists, highly respected for their knowledge and involvement in the ethics field, five percent admitted to using "client welfare or other deeper values" as a rationale for engaging in sex with a client (Jennings et al., 2005).

Some might argue that the pendulum has swung too far; therapists, athletic coaches, and even preschool teachers are concerned that the slightest physical contact might lead to accusations of inappropriate touching. In this regard, it seems crucial to "know thy patient," that is, we must carefully assess a patient to understand where their boundaries lie. For one client, being comforted by a hand clasp might be viewed as quite appropriate under certain circumstances, while another client may feel that such behavior is intrusive, and yet a third may actually welcome the contact, hoping that it will lead to further intimate behavior.

It is also important for therapists to "know themselves" as well as their patients. The therapeutic situation can present opportunities for exploitation that are difficult to resist — particularly if one's own romantic needs are not being met. We must be vigilant for warning signs that tell us we may be moving toward inappropriateness. In reviewing dozens of cases that came before ethical committees, it was found that almost always the "the act of sexual intimacy was the culmination of a lengthy process that started with vague, uneasy feelings of excitement, but progressed in tidy, rationalized steps" (Keith-Spiegel & Koocher, 1985).

> Dr. Hotandbothered had been treating Johanna during a period in which his marriage was under severe strain. His wife had left the workforce and had returned to school to pursue a master's degree in nursing. Her program was quite intense, requiring that she often

work at nights and on weekends at the college clinic. Johanna had been raised in a rather oppressive home environment and had learned early from her father that she was to be "seen but not heard." Now for the first time in her life she had met a man (her therapist) who really listened to her and seemed to appreciate and value her as a person. Romantic expressions began innocently enough — a hug after emotional sessions, more and more time spent discussing nontherapy-related topics and the doctor's personal life. When Johanna asked about his schedule and then booked a last appointment of the evening (something she had never done before), it was clear that things had gotten out of hand. At the following session, the therapist addressed the issue by stating that they would need to return to a therapeutic focus. She, however, felt betrayed by yet another man and terminated therapy. Not only had a client been lost, but Johanna, who had come to therapy with one set of problems, now had additional issues to resolve.

❖ Avoiding the Error

1. Recognize that not meeting relationship and romantic needs outside of one's clinical practice leaves a therapist vulnerable to inappropriate boundary crossing.

2. Take immediate action when either you or the client seems to be engaging in boundary-crossing behavior. Remind yourself that the greatest number of complaints and suspensions to psychological boards involve violations of physical intimacy guidelines.

3. Be aware of seductive statements or gestures and ask yourself (a) What does the client get by being seductive? and (b) What needs would the client be meeting if the seduction was successful or unsuccessful? Some common issues when a client is being seductive include
    a. As a result of sharing deep personal material, the client confuses romantic and personal intimacy.
    b. The client is desperately seeking physical intimacy and feels closest emotionally to the therapist.
    c. The client wants or needs more control of the therapeutic situation and is using sex as a way to gain that control.

d. The client senses (or misconstrues) the therapist's needs and attempts to satisfy them.
e. The client has a need to undermine the therapist or the therapeutic process.

❖ *Error #28*

Having Boundaries That Are Too Rigid

...emotionally distant therapists can be as dangerous as those that seek too much intimacy.
— M. Webster (1991)

At the other end of the spectrum from fusion is "individuation" — a state in which therapists maintain a considerable emotional distance from their clients. These therapists seem "tuned out" and are therefore viewed as cold, aloof, and uncaring. When this is the case, therapeutic effectiveness is diminished, and clients are very likely to terminate unilaterally.

To keep one's emotional distance when hearing of a patient's distress or past trauma is a natural response. Any moviegoer has observed how children and adults alike often avert their eyes at particularly gruesome or dramatic moments. How much greater is the tendency to avoid the discomfort of hearing about the real life dramas and traumas our patients have endured? The problem is that by becoming detached the therapist is likely to act and speak in ways that may minimize the gravity of the patient's experiences. This can lead to patients feeling misunderstood or even blameworthy for their misfortune.

Detached therapists may also move to cut off a patient's strong feelings before they have been fully expressed. It is certainly every therapist's goal to reduce emotional pain and suffering; and yet sometimes it is therapeutically necessary to revisit memories, events, and images that are painful. Our natural tendency at such times is to attempt to assuage the pain — perhaps by changing the subject or immediately reaching for the Kleenex box. This is certainly appropriate if the client is sending clear signals of dissociation; however, we need to keep in mind that one of the curative factors in therapy is for the client to reach a place where recollections of a painful past can be gradually tolerated. Thus we can actually impede therapeutic progress when we cut off these strong feelings too soon, preventing clients from mustering their own coping strategies.

❖**Avoiding the Error**

1. After each clinical session, take a few minutes to recharge emotionally. Even if pressed for time, it is best to change the focus by doing something pleasant and even playful, such as a short "nonbusiness" phone call or e-mail.

2. Allow the client to vent appropriate emotions. This does not mean reinforcing histrionics but rather giving permission to fully express genuine and perhaps previously unrecognized feelings.

3. Remind the client that even though you may not have experienced the identical situation in your life, you can certainly recognize the distress the patient experienced.

4. Thank the patient for trusting you by sharing her or his intimate past.

❖ *Error #29*

Making Inappropriate Levels of Therapist Self-Disclosure

The therapist conceals behind an impervious mask his or her private life, who he or she really is. Like the moon, the therapist reflects back ... the patient's expectations of other people.

— W. Myers (1982)

Freudians say no to it — "it will ruin the blank screen upon which feelings can be projected and negate transference." Others object to it because it could adversely affect treatment outcome by exposing the therapist's weaknesses or vulnerabilities, reducing the client's trust in the therapist. The "it" is therapist self-disclosure. And pro- and anti-disclosure proponents have been debating the issue for decades. Fortunately, recent scientific research has provided a much needed factual basis to this debate.

The most comprehensive study of therapist self-disclosure was undertaken by Barrett and Berman (2001). They trained therapists in reciprocal self-disclosure, that is, disclosures that matched the topic and intensity of the client's disclosures. For example, if a client disclosed feeling upset about a relationship breakup, the therapist would reveal similar experiences and feelings. The results were dramatic. Clients whose therapists engaged in reciprocal self-disclosure reported less symptom distress and they also liked their therapists more than those whose therapists were judged as low disclosers.

This research validates earlier studies that showed when therapists self-disclose, clients are more likely to see them as friendly, open, helpful, and warm. However, there is one important caution. The average number of therapist disclosures in the experimental group was slightly over five per session, whereas the average number of client disclosures was sixty. In addition, therapist disclosures were considerably briefer than those of the client. This means that therapists did not respond in a "tit for tat" manner to every disclosure of the client's but were quite judicious in their personal expressions. Too many disclosures could actually have a negative impact on treatment in that clients might not have enough time to express themselves and might also feel overwhelmed by too many details of the therapist's own personal history.

❖ Avoiding the Error

1. Keep therapist disclosures succinct and relevant. If the client's "story" takes five minutes, the therapist-related experience should be much briefer.

2. Try to match the intimacy and emotional intensity of the disclosure.

   A counselor intern at a college counseling center listened to his client describe her relationship problems with her father, who she viewed as rigid and lacking in understanding of the difficulties of student life. She felt that her roommates all had more sensitive, involved, and supportive fathers. The therapist, trying to demonstrate understanding, merely said, "Yes, I don't like my father very much either, and I stay away as much as I can." The client was aghast and changed the subject, becoming distant. In supervision, the counselor realized that he had tried to show empathy, but his statement was likely viewed as minimizing the significance of his client's intimate disclosure.

❖ *Error #30*

Failing to Set Boundaries for Out-of-Session Client-Therapist Contact

Many clients attempt to have more out of session contact than is appropriate within a therapeutic relationship. This can be by phone, by requests that the therapist come to special events like weddings, or, due to today's technology, by e-mail:

> A therapist intern seemed quite proud while describing the strong bond she had developed with a client: "She e-mails me at least once a day to get my advice and has given me a number of thank you notes for always being there for her." Unfortunately, a closer inspection of the "therapeutic relationship" revealed that the therapist was actually exacerbating this patient's dependency needs by providing guidance on matters that the client needed to think through on her own. For example, the client had agreed to call a parks and recreation program to get information on joining a basketball league. She was provided with two numbers by the information line but could not decide which number to call and e-mailed the therapist for assistance. This pattern of seeking help for rather uncomplicated decision making began to increase day by day.

Clearly this type of easy access to a therapist can encourage dependency on the therapist and inhibit the process of developing independent decision making on the part of the client. Obviously, the goal for therapists is to teach clients how to satisfy their needs for themselves. Out-of-session contact, especially when it is to reduce anxiety, can all too often become an addiction, with all the problems associated with addictive behavior, including anger if the addicting substance (the therapist) is not available when the dependency urge is present.

❖ Avoiding the Error

1. Be aware when a request for contact merely serves the function of reducing anxiety, especially about a decision the client needs to make or an action that is being contemplated.

2. Clearly define the limits of outside contact. Clarify that phone calls are for emergencies only. Occasionally the term *emergency* has to be narrowly defined with some clients who have a broader view of what constitutes an urgent need.

3. In order to maintain a buffer between your personal and professional life, never provide a client with your home or personal cell phone number, no matter how important you think the issue is.

4. Be judicious about internet contact. The internet is not a secure medium, and according to HIPPA regulations such use can violate client privacy rights (Mallen, Vogel, & Rochlen, 2005).

How to Guarantee Noncompliance with Assignments

A meta-analysis of 27 studies showed that both homework assignments and homework compliance are positively related to psychotherapy outcome.

— N. Kazantzis, F. Deane, and K. R. Ronan (2000)

As the Kazantzis, Deane, and Ronan study indicates, providing clients with opportunities to apply what they have learned in therapy is one of the keys to therapeutic effectiveness. This makes good sense, given that clients only spend an hour or two per week in therapy and 165+ hours in the real world. So it would stand to reason that the majority of therapists would regularly utilize "out-of-session" activities as part of their therapeutic arsenal. However, the sad truth is that the majority of therapists report never using such assignments. Why would there be this disconnection between what the research shows and what most therapists do?

What the research doesn't show is that creating homework assignments that clients actually comply with is a tricky business — and there is a multitude of therapeutic errors that can interfere with the process.

A case history will help illustrate:

Dr. Doomed was working with a young woman, Sabrina, who he diagnosed as socially phobic. Sabrina had particular difficulty in her college classes, worrying excessively about bringing attention to herself. To avoid the possibility of embarrassment she always arrived early to class, sat in the last row, and never raised her hand. After several weeks of therapy in which no assignments were made, the therapist decided it was time for action and suggested that Sabrina arrive five minutes late to her next class meeting. At her next session, Sabrina at first told her therapist that she forgot to do the assignment but later admitted that she was able to comply with the first part of the assignment — being late — but could not muster the courage to actually enter the classroom, so she ended up cutting class.

Was Sabrina's case just another example of client "resistance," lack of commitment, or readiness to change? In fact, a careful analysis of the approach used by the therapist reveals several therapeutic errors that greatly decrease the likelihood of compliance.

Error #31

Developing the "Out of Session Activity" Unilaterally

For starters, Dr. Doom "decided" on his own, without input from his client, that it was time for action, and then he chose what that action should be. This one-sided approach helped guarantee noncompliance. Just as the entire therapeutic process should be collaborative, each assignment needs to be arrived at by a joint meeting of the minds. Thus, the term "assignment" is not really appropriate at all, because it connotes one person doing the "assigning" and the other person complying. Far better are concepts such as "experiments," "activities," or "tasks." Therapists certainly can take the lead in developing possible strategies, but clients must be encouraged to provide their input and feedback as the tasks are developed. Clients who feel they have participated in the process of generating the activity are more likely to attempt it, complete it, and maintain whatever they have learned from it. Leaving the client out of the decision-making process increases the likelihood that the task may be beyond the reach of the client's capabilities. In this case, suggesting the client arrive late to class was an attempt to hit a "home run" with one pitch, instead of moving gradually toward the ultimate goal.

❖Avoiding the Error

1. Use a "brainstorming " approach by participating with the client in developing two or three possible outside activities which

might help reduce the problem. Next, put these solutions in order ranging from least to most difficult. In the case of the socially phobic college student, sitting a little closer to the front of the class (instead of in the farthest reaches of the room) might be the easiest task; arriving five minutes early (instead of ten) might be moderately difficult, and arriving late would be the most difficult.

2. Allow the client to make the determination of which activity should be attempted initially. Remember, activities do not have to be highly difficult in order for them to be valuable.

3. Be careful not to sway the client in the direction of the activity that you would prefer be undertaken. This is particularly important in the case of passive individuals who are particularly prone to pleasing their therapists.

> A client who engaged in a high level of compliance with the wishes of others and a very low level of making her own needs known, was helped to generate two possible homework assignments: one of these would be completed at work, and the other with her friends. Both tasks were assessed to be equivalently difficult, and approximately equally anxiety provoking, but the client "intuited" which one the therapist favored and agreed to do the work-oriented assignment. The following week the assignment had not been initiated, nor was it the week after. The therapist (wisely) questioned the client about the other alternative and found that it was really the client's first choice, but she had chosen the other because she did not want to disappoint the therapist.

4. Reinforce the client for providing input and decision making. Adults, children, dogs, employees, and clients all respond to praise with a tendency to repeat the desired behavior. As noted child psychologist Haim Ginott said, "Catch them being good."

❖ *Error #32*

Failing to Adequately Prepare Clients for the "Assignment"

All too often, clinicians employ a "take two aspirin and stay out of drafts" approach to therapy. That is, they act as if mental health work is identical to the medical model in which clients ask the "all-knowing" physician for a diagnosis, prognosis, and treatment recommendations. In reality, most therapy clients need to be persuaded of the efficacy of specific interventions. In this case, not only was Sabrina's input not sought, nowhere in the course of Dr. Doomed's assignment-giving was there even a clue as to what this fear-inducing activity was supposed to accomplish. What might have seemed obvious to the therapist was probably not at all clear to the client. For those with phobias such as Sabrina's, education about the efficacy of "gradual exposure" should have preceded any specific homework recommendations. Preparation for homework compliance also entails a thorough assessment of the obstacles that might prevent compliance. Remember, if it was easy for clients to engage in these behaviors, they probably already would be doing so. As the following case demonstrates, an inspection of these barriers can help the therapist and client understand the underlying problem more clearly.

> A 34-year-old female client who worked in the human relations department of a microprocessing company complained about her present job and the previous one as well, where she worked for "Mr. Evil." The present job was overwhelming, requiring her to take work home, which left her no time or energy to connect with her "neglected" husband. However, because there had also been problems in the previous job, the therapist began to wonder if she was contributing to her own occupational difficulties.

Thus, oblivious to what the client had said about being overwhelmed, the therapist got her to agree to "journal" about her feelings toward her current job. The following week, no journaling had occurred, so to make the assignment easier, the client agreed to tape record her thoughts. At the next session, feeling ever guiltier she confessed that she could not find her tape recorder. Finally, the therapist came to his senses and decided to further inspect the barriers to completing the assignment. From that discussion it became clear that the client did not need to journal her feelings, instead, she needed to find a job that could allow her "time to breathe," let alone make journal entries. She then decided to ask for a transfer to a less taxing position in the company she worked for.

❖**Avoiding the Error**

1. Assume nothing — all too often therapists "assign" activities such as journal writing, relaxation, and imagery techniques, with no explanation, assuming that the benefits of such activities will be obvious to a client who will be happily compliant with the therapist's wishes.

2. Allow sufficient time within the session to develop appropriate assignments and to assess potential obstacles. Last minute recommendations such as was the case with Sabrina are likely to fall on deaf ears.

❖ *Error #33*

Failing to Provide Backup Support to Increase Compliance

Having clients comply with homework (even those assignments they have helped design) is about as difficult as getting students to complete school assignments on time. Understanding this, successful therapists utilize a wide array of approaches designed to overcome the numerous obstacles to completing out-of-session activities.

❖**Avoiding the Error**

1. Use "Post-It® notes." At the conclusion of a session, suggest that the client write down the assignment and then post it at home in a convenient location. The therapist should also make a note of the assignment so it can be reviewed at the next session.

2. Encourage the client to tell a trusted individual about the task, asking the friend to check back and see how the assignment is going. This person should not be a "guilt inducer" or have any vested interest in the activity other than the welfare of the client. Typically spouses, children, and parents are not useful choices.

3. Determine if the client has a "buddy" who is also willing to engage in the desired activity. This can be especially helpful

with assignments such as increased exercise or attending classes or support groups.

4. Frame the assignments as a way to learn about oneself while trying new things. Emphasize the possibility of enjoying the opportunity to develop new skills that could be beneficial for a lifetime. This is the "salesperson" component of being a therapist.

5. Leave little or nothing to chance by carefully clarifying the how, when, and where components of the assignment.

6. Utilize a formal assessment tool such as the HRS (Kazantzis et al., 2000). This instrument attempts to identify specific barriers that can impede compliance with out-of-session activities. The HRS contains twelve questions that clients complete each week immediately prior to their session. Questions explore client, therapist, and task factors. The client factor explores how well the rationale for the assignment was understood and how much the assignment was enjoyed.

Although most therapists will not employ such a tool with every assignment, periodic use of HRS-like questions can be invaluable in helping the clinician and client identify barriers preventing assignment completion and thus therapeutic growth. Therapists can also gain valuable feedback concerning their ability to provide clear rationales, specific guidelines, and tasks with appropriate levels of challenge.

How to Make Bad Attitudes Worse

No psychological problem can be solved, no helping process can be conducted without attempts to change attitudes.

— D. Johnson (1980)

How many times have you heard parents exhort their children by saying, "You need to change your attitude young man (or woman)." Therapists often experience the same frustration: "Why can't my client see how harmful and distorted their self-defeating attitudes are and just get over them?" If only it were that easy. Yet, the hard work of changing client attitudes can be the heart and soul of therapeutic work. Negative attitudes are direct contributors to feelings of depression, anger, anxiety, shame, and guilt. But as all therapists know, attitudes can be highly resistant to change. Clients cling relentlessly to self-defeating attitudes, such as feeling they are "inferior" or "unattractive," even in the face of significant evidence to the contrary. Attitude change requires examination of a client's views of the self, the world, and the future. Many of these cognitions were developed over a period of years and can be deeply entrenched. Thus, attitude change is a tricky business and doing so requires awareness of those therapeutic errors that can actually strengthen the very attitudes you wish to modify

As a first step, it is crucial for therapists to understand the distinction between attitudes and cognitions. Simple cognitions are clear responses to very specific contexts. An example is a student who feels that one or two teachers do not like him (which may or may not be true). Attitudes, on the other hand, are grand summaries of a wide variety of related cognitions that have developed in a number of contexts, resulting in attitudes such as

"People in authority never like me." People state their cognitions directly. However, people rarely state an attitude directly, rather they express them through patterns of statements around a particular theme.

For example

1. "People are untrustworthy" is an attitude reflecting distrust across various situations involving relationships with friends, the opposite sex, family members, or employers. Statements of cognitions such as "I don't like to talk about myself" or "Friendships are not that important to me" may reflect such an attitude.

2. "I will fail at everything" is an attitude that manifests itself when the person is called upon to undertake new tasks. Individuals with this attitude may state, "This assignment is impossible" or "I never measure up."

3. "I am basically unlikable" is an attitude that rears its ugly head when the person is facing possible rejection. Thus when meeting anyone for the first time they might state, "This will probably be another disaster."

Compared to attitudes, cognitions are easier for clients and therapists to recognize as they occur. This allows for the implementation of cognitive therapy, which has proven very beneficial in helping clients identify a variety of distorted and unproductive thought patterns. The "how to's" of cognitive therapy have been comprehensively dealt with in dozens of popular technical publications. However, approaches to attitude change have received significantly less attention, and a number of therapeutic errors are commonly made when attempting to modify client attitudes.

Error #34

Failing to Prepare the Client for Attitude Change

Too often therapists launch into disputes over a client's attitudes without laying the groundwork for doing so. When this is the case, the client can feel attacked without warning, often leading to a hardening of the viewpoint as the client attempts to argue the case. Avoiding this scenario means first of all explaining the relationship between attitudes and emotions; that is, "Negative attitudes often result in negative emotions," and therefore modifying emotions means examining an attitude's logical basis.

> A fourth-year student at a two-year college complained that he had been feeling down lately because all of his friends are further along toward graduating than he is. He had to repeat a math course, and to help out his parents financially he dropped out for a semester so he could work full time. Before countering his attitude that he is "inferior" because of less educational attainment, the therapist first explains the consequences of this attitude: "We have been discussing the connection between the fact that you have been feeling down lately and the attitude that you are not as competent as your friends who are moving through college more quickly. Is the connection somewhat clear? If so, do you think it would be useful to examine the possibility that being behind is really not such a bad thing?"

Once the client understands the connection between the attitude and his negative feelings, the therapist can move into the appropriate attitude change procedure.

❖ Avoiding the Error

1. Realize that as therapists we have read numerous treatises on the idea of the relationship between thoughts and behavior. However, to the average client, this concept is probably somewhat foreign. Thus a careful "connecting the dots" must occur in order for the client to "join" in the pursuit of a new, more productive attitude. Otherwise, prepare for a battle of wits.

2. Use humor rather than a "corrective professorial" approach to make your point. "There goes that 'all-or-none attitude' again that we love so much" is better than a stern reminder that the client is once again using "distorted" thinking.

3. Don't simply try to talk a client out of an attitude. It is bigger than both of you. Only action, experience, and imagery are powerful enough to modify attitudes.

❖ *Error #35*

Relying on Passive Learning Strategies

Attitude change does not occur by lecture, exhortation, or a "you can do it" pep talk. Merely telling clients with low self-esteem that they actually have quite a few positive attributes, interests, and skills is unlikely to do the trick. Instead, therapists need to do what great teachers have done since ancient times — actively involve students in the learning process. And attitude change is a learning process very similar to that of learning a new philosophy or set of values. Active learning has been shown to result in much greater internalization of concepts than passive rote learning.

❖Avoiding the Error

1. Utilize Socratic questioning. This approach is as old as Socrates — perhaps even more ancient. Rather than lecturing clients as to why they should change inappropriate attitudes, Socratic questioning, which is systematic and nonconfrontational, allows people to draw their own conclusions about the inaccuracy of their negative attitudes. Matross (1975) developed a four-step approach in which he applied the Socratic method to alter unhealthy attitudes clients had toward themselves:
   a. Identify the unhealthy attitude. First the therapist does a careful assessment to elicit any negative attitudes such as "I have not accomplished much in life," "I am incompetent," "I have failed at everything."
   b. Identify an alternative attitude — one incompatible with the negative one. Following assessment, the therapist constructs a view of the client that is more positive and accurate; e.g., "I am more competent than I think."
   c. Elicit several examples of behaviors associated with the incompatible attitude. Now the questioning begins in order to reveal inconsistencies with the unhealthy attitude:
      ❖ Can you think of a couple of examples, recently or in the past, when you put some effort into accomplishing something?

❖ What were the results of your effort?

❖ How did you feel about the outcome?

❖ What response did you receive for your work?

   d. Lead the client to consider the new incompatible attitude. The final step is to help the client summarize the "competing" information and integrate it into a revised self-view, "Based on what we have been talking about, what are your thoughts about your ability to be successful at times."

2. Role play. Using this approach the therapist explains to the client how sometimes the most effective way to change a harmful attitude is to "practice acting as if you are a person whose attitude is the opposite of yours, for example, someone with high levels of confidence who enjoys talking about his strengths and accomplishments." It is crucial that the therapist encourage the client to fully insert himself into the role because "the more emotionally involved [the client] gets in the role play, the more effect it will have on his attitudes" (Johnson, 1980).

❖
Error #36

Failing to Attend to the Client's Core Beliefs

Alex, a 32-year-old client, was in the middle of his third marriage (or should we say toward the end of it) when his wife insisted he come to therapy with her to address his feelings of distrust toward her. Inspection of his previous romantic relationships revealed a deeply held attitude that women were untrustworthy. This led him to engage in "distance-seeking" behavior, with the "self-fulfilling" result that his partners — including his wife — grew ever more disengaged from him. Initially, the therapist attempted to apply cognitive change techniques aimed at reducing Alex's "black-and-white" thinking and tendency to generalize. The client agreed intellectually, but this did nothing to change his basic feelings toward women. After being referred to another therapist more schooled in attitude change, Alex began to recognize after a time that the attitude underlying his difficulties involved believing that women are untrustworthy because men will ultimately disappoint them, just as his father had done. When the focus shifted to the correct core belief, appropriate attitude change techniques were applied and Alex made significant progress.

Deeply held beliefs are changeable, but only when clearly identified and only when the client can be brought to see what these beliefs produce and that other admirable and successful people hold other beliefs that aid more on life's path.

❖ Avoiding the Error

1. To gain insight into what clients believe, ask about people that the client admires or looks up to:
   a. What heroes or heroines in books, films, or life did you admire as a child?
   b. Who are your heroes now?
   c. What news story about someone's actions has raised your spirits?

2. Inspect what clients think their heroes or mentors believe. Are these beliefs the client shares? When there is a difference, why is that so?
   a. What do you think these people believe?
   b. Do you share the same beliefs?
   c. Who would you want as a life teacher?
   d. What would you learn from your life teacher?

3. Form a more comprehensive picture of the role the belief plays in the client's life by asking
   a. What does this belief gain for you?
   b. What does this belief protect you from?
   c. What does it cost you?
   d. Is the cost too high?
   e. What else can a happy, reasonable person believe?

Remember core beliefs do not pop up on one occasion or in response to a one-time series of questions. Values assessment is an ongoing and integral part of the therapeutic process.

❖ *Error #37*

Failing to Explain That Attitudes Are Not Fixed Traits

Why am I so depressed? — it must be my personality — other people don't let things bother them the way I do.

The way clients view the source of their problems can have a considerable impact on their level of optimism for change. When they see their problems as resulting from stable and fixed sources, such as their basic personality or the "fates," they are likely to feel hopeless and demoralized. Thus, therapists must modify these misperceptions by shaping explanations that center on the role of environmental stresses and learned habits of behavior and thinking. Ascribing problems to unstable sources can provide at least short-term improvement in client well-being as well as hope for long-term change.

During her first appointment, Rosie, a 59-year-old office manager living in California, stated that she had ruined her relationship with her brother, her last living relative. She had gone to a wedding in Wisconsin where he lived and entered into a discussion with her brother's wife of forty-five years. The discussion turned argumentative, and Rosie was adamant that she was much more knowledgeable on the subject and his wife was ignorant of the facts. As a consequence, her brother stated that he would no longer visit her in the summer as he and his wife had done for decades. The underlying attitude that led to Rosie's difficulties was summarized by her statement to her therapist that "I have always believed that if someone is wrong, you simply tell them so." An inspection of those people in her life that she valued revealed that both her father and her husband supported such an attitude, believing that "silence is equivalent to assent." At this point, Rosie believed that there was no way for her to change since throughout her life she had lost numerous relationships because of her strong opinions. Initially, the therapist tried to utilize a cognitive approach wherein Rosie was to consider the relative merits of stating her opinion on matters to her brother's wife or salvaging the relationship with her last family member. Even though Rosie could logically understand that the higher value was her relationship with her brother, she still could not see herself avoiding a blowup. To help modify the idea that change was possible, the therapist had her practice the statement "I strongly disagree with you, but it is not worth the argument" and then imagined herself leaving the room. Ultimately, Rosie felt she could handle an interaction with her brother's wife who was now seen as the one incapable of change.

❖ Avoiding the Error

1. Have clients who see themselves as unchangeable learn something new for the next session. This can be as simple as learning to cook something different or attempting a crossword puzzle if they have never done so.

2. Engage the client in a discussion that reviews the various adjustments they have made in life such as attending new schools, moving from one area to another, and making new friends. Remind the client how difficult and seemingly insurmountable these adjustments might have seemed at first but over time became a source of pride and accomplishment.

3. Discuss the concepts of "optimism" and "pessimism." Have the client identify where on a continuum they currently view themselves, their future, their world view. Have them chart their optimism quotient weekly, noting any changes that occur.

How Not to Confront Clients

Confrontation is used when the therapist detects discrepancies
(a) between what the clients are saying and what they have
said before, (b) between what the clients are communicating
verbally and nonverbally, and (c) between the way the clients
view their problem and the way the therapist views it.

— S. R. Walen, R. DiGiueseppe,
and W. Dryden (1992)

It is a rare therapist who relishes the idea of pointing out a client's inconsistencies, deficits, and negative behavioral or cognitive patterns. By and large we want to nurture, encourage, and empathize, while emphasizing a person's strengths. Thus, we often avoid discussing our clients' repeated tardiness to sessions, their delinquent payments, their self-defeating behaviors, and their noncompliance with agreed-on therapeutic assignments. All too often bringing up such matters is viewed as *confrontational* — a term that evokes images of tense verbal battles in which one party tries to get the upper hand. However, the goal of therapeutic confrontations is quite different. Rather than being a power play, it is an attempt to educate and expand the client's self-awareness.

❖ *Error #38*

Responding Passively to the Client's Unproductive Behaviors

A client at a college counseling center began therapy with some misgivings in that her previous therapist had discontinued treatment with only the vague assertion that he didn't feel he could help her. Her new therapist was troubled by numerous behaviors that were seen as "therapy avoidant." That is, she often came late to sessions, left sessions early to attend other activities, and missed sessions without calling in advance. Interestingly, the missed sessions often occurred after a particularly "effective" therapy meeting, at least from the therapist's point of view. The therapist was afraid that if he raised these issues, he might lose the client and, even worse, fail as a therapist with a case he had worked on for an extended period.

Many therapists who avoid confrontation are just not comfortable in an authoritative or assertive role. This is somewhat analogous to the parent who is quite good at the nurturing component of parenting but who finds it difficult to set appropriate limits. Of course patients are not children, but there are times when assertive communications are the life blood of therapy — the chance for therapeutic growth. To omit such communications is equivalent to letting children raise themselves without parental guidance.

In the case of the "therapy-avoidant" patient mentioned above, the therapist was helped to formulate an assertive response. He told his client that he wanted very much for therapy to be successful but that he wondered whether she might be more comfortable and thus consistent with another therapist. He then asked the client if that would be a good solution and if not, "what might be?" This "confrontation" led to a productive discussion in which the client became aware of her "ambivalence" about connecting with yet another therapist, fearful that she might be abandoned again. At the end of the "confrontation," the client stated that she was actually astonished that the therapist cared enough about her to discuss this issue, and this led to a renewed commitment to therapy.

❖ Avoiding the Error

1. Recognize that clients will rarely respond negatively to "confrontations" if they are delivered with sensitivity.

2. Proceed cautiously by balancing any criticism with supportive statements as well. As in the case history cited above, the therapist was careful to state first and foremost that he was seeking a successful outcome for the client, not that he was admonishing her for her apparent lack of commitment to

therapy. He then proceeded to question whether her lateness to sessions might be a reflection of her dissatisfaction with treatment.

3. When faced with bringing up tough issues, behaviorally rehearse the statements in advance until reasonably comfortable. In other words, we need to "take our own medicine," and practice assertive behaviors in advance in order to reduce anxiety.

4. Remind yourself that therapy involves providing a balance of compassion and challenge to clients. To focus only on the nurturing aspects of the therapeutic endeavor is to omit the basis for therapeutic growth — and that is *change*. And change does not typically occur out of thin air — it often requires a therapist who cares enough to address the client's negative or unproductive patterns of behavior or thinking.

Error #39

Responding in an Aggressive or Insensitive Way

At the other extreme from passive therapists are those whose feedback is presented in an overly stern or harsh manner. Such therapists seem to forget a fundamental tenet of "assertiveness training": When sending negatives, communications must be firm enough to make the point, while at the same time being respectful and supportive.

> A case in point involved a college professor who was having an affair with a married colleague. Patiently she had waited several years for him to leave his wife, but he always provided one excuse or another for not ending the marriage. Her therapist was getting as tired as she was with the situation and was desperate to get it resolved. In a moment of impatience, he stated, "Have you ever given any thought at all to how this might impact his wife and children?" The client was greatly offended by this attempt at guilt induction, and terminated therapy abruptly.

Every therapist has a "breaking point." Sometimes it is a particular type of client who can trigger insensitive or hostile comments. These can include teenagers who endlessly complain about their parents, divorcing couples who involve their children in the breakup, abusive parents, clients unwilling to try anything out of their comfort zone, and couples who see only their spouse's contribution to their marital problems. These are but a few of the many types of cases that can challenge a therapist's patience and goodwill. What clinician hasn't wanted to tell a complaining teenager that his parents are humans also and are just trying to do their job? What pleasure it might bring to remind overly protective parents that they were once young themselves? However, the pleasure of such confrontations would most likely be offset by an ever-diminishing caseload.

❖ Avoiding the Error

1. Identify those categories of patients who are likely to push your buttons. In addition to those listed above, some therapists have little tolerance for "ADHD-type" clients who can't seem to stay on the subject at hand, highly shy individuals who continually have to be drawn into conversation, narcissistic clients for whom all is "about them," borderline clients who are unpredictable and often attack the therapist, and depressed clients when they are in a particularly "whiney" mood.

2. Be firm in establishing appropriate rules for behavior during therapy. This is particularly important during couples or family sessions.

3. Let clients know directly and honestly that their behavior is not conducive to the goals of therapy. Sometimes a gentle metaphor such as the following can be useful to convey the message: "Now this is where I feel like I need to give you a kick in the butt. This is about you taking care of yourself, and what you're telling me is you don't take care of yourself. So I want to give you a kick in the butt" (Kassan, 1999).

How to Get Clients to Refuse Medication

Having a therapist suggests the possibility of a medication consultation ... and taking pills to alter the way in which one thinks or feels are all part of an interaction which may have powerful meanings for the patient.

— M. Gitlin (1996)

Amber, a 23-year-old student, had returned to school after having been hospitalized following a severe manic episode. She sought treatment at her college psychological counseling center where she stated that her "episodes" were now controlled fairly well with medication but that she still felt somewhat depressed and was having difficulty establishing relationships on campus. After consulting with her psychiatrist, a recommendation was made that she add an antidepressant to her medication regimen. However, Amber was adamantly opposed to this idea stating, "I don't want to be overmedicated and dependent on drugs."

In spite of the common perception that masses of people seek relief from psychological symptoms through medication, the reality is that making medication recommendations is one of the most treacherous and delicate interventions a therapist can undertake. This is clearly exemplified in Amber's case. Here is someone whose medication experience is essentially positive, and yet she is highly resistant to adding a second medication. For those who have never utilized psychotropic medication, the resistance can be even greater. In many cases, unless adequate preparation and sensitivity are employed, the therapist-client relationship can be damaged or premature unilateral termination can occur.

Error #40

Failing to Prepare Clients in Advance for the Possibility of Medication

Knowing that most clients are going to resist the idea of medication, it is best to sow the seeds for this possibility as early in treatment as possible. Therapists begin to develop a sixth sense that their patients' symptoms might be severe enough to warrant a medication evaluation. When this is the case, it is useful to mention that sometimes therapy is enhanced by the use of medication. Be careful to emphasize that you are not sure yet whether it will be appropriate in this case. Then try to elicit the patient's attitudes toward the possibility of using medication. This will give you an idea of what you might be up against down the road.

❖Avoiding the Error

1. Assess the client's prior history with psychotropic medication early in therapy as well as the client's present attitudes toward medication use.

2. Continually update your knowledge about psychopharmacology. This can be accomplished by attendance at continuing education courses, by "visiting" online web sites such as Medline, and by keeping up to date with the literature.

3. When dealing with disorders where medication is commonly utilized, inform your clients of this early in treatment. Provide them with a brief but factual basis for the medication's possible effectiveness.

4. Develop a list of potential referrals for medication evaluations. Be careful to base your recommendations on the testimonials of former or current patients rather than recommending those clinicians with whom you have a personal relationship.

Error #41

❖

Failing to Be Prepared for Client Objections, Concerns, and Resistance to Medication

An accountant for an oil company was displaying signs of vegetative depression (disturbed sleeping patterns, reduced appetite, clumsiness, and some psychomotor retardation). The therapist correctly suggested a psychiatric consult for possible medication. The client agreed with a nod of the head but then put off the appointment, and when it was finally made missed it by oversleeping.

When a recommendation for a medication evaluation is made, it is important to actively solicit any concerns the patient may have. In the case cited above, the therapist had mistaken the client's slight nod of the head for a commitment to seeking a medication evaluation. Only weeks later, after the client had missed the appointment, did the therapist more thoroughly investigate any reservations the client had about the referral. Then it was discovered that confidentiality was the main issue. It seems the client's employer processed insurance claims "in house," and he did not wish to have it noted in his record that he was receiving medical treatment for a psychiatric illness.

❖**Avoiding the Error**

1. When possible, talk about the use of medication in general terms before recommending to clients that they get a psychiatric consultation.

2. Do not confuse client silence for assent. Some clients may be quite passive and not willing to risk their therapist's disapproval by questioning the therapist's recommendations. In these cases, it is the therapist's job to elicit possible objections by posing a question such as "Many people have strong concerns about the use of medication as part of therapy — I wonder whether you have any?"

3. Be prepared to answer clients' questions and help them reduce their anxiety around this issue. Oftentimes, resistance to

medication is related to the meanings that patients attach to the idea of being medicated. Below are some of the more common objections or concerns patients may raise and some suggested responses to these concerns:

Patient: Does this mean that you are dissatisfied with my progress in therapy?

Therapist: Not at all. It means that therapy can be assisted and made faster by a temporary adjustment of brain chemistry.

Patient: Does this mean you think I am crazy or just not healthy enough for regular therapy?

Therapist: Medication is usually a temporary boost that helps our "talk" therapy work faster. Once you get depressed or anxious, your brain can settle into a new pattern that becomes habitual. Medication can help you get out of that habit and back to a more adaptive state.

For many patients, the concerns are the result of an information gap. They are justifiably worried about issues such as addiction and side effects. In such cases, a psychoeducational approach is appropriate. This can involve a wide variety of educational tools, including brochures, web sites, and visual aids that help explain basic concepts of brain function. (Two helpful websites which provide good overviews for laypersons of psychotropic medications are *Healthyplace.com* and *askthetherapist.com.*)

Client: I just read about terrible side effects of anti-depressants.

Therapist: Side effects do happen and bad ones make the news. They are uncommon, but the physician I referred you to is quite willing to discuss this in detail and also tell you how to spot any signs of difficulties.

Client: I still would rather not take the chance.

Therapist: That's fine. But you should at least talk to an expert about this and make an informed decision. If after the consult you don't want to try medication, you don't have to. If the psychiatrist agrees you are a good candidate for medication and can allay your fears, you have one more option to feel better.

Medication is a tool to assist in the process of therapy. For the right person at the right time it can aid and speed treatment. Neither an automatic *yes* nor an automatic *no* are good answers to the recommendation for a medication consult. Clients should always be reminded that they are in charge of the treatment, and a consult means neither that medication will be prescribed nor that if prescribed the client should take it. It's merely an option that can aid treatment.

How Not to Terminate Therapy

Out of the nature of the work comes the nature of the closing. If we've met for three times, we might stop and we might terminate in the same session that the idea of termination comes up. If we've been meeting for three years, we'll probably be talking about it over time. We'll probably be tapering off for a while and then talking about the nature of the relationship.

— M. Sullivan, T. Skovhold, and L. Jennings (2005)

Beginnings of relationships are always hard: the first moments of contact with a new client are a "make it or break it" time as we try to bridge that awkward gap between strangers. Endings can be even more difficult: sometimes clients become the "disappeared" — unilaterally terminating without warning. Even when the decision is mutual, feelings of loss can arise for both client and therapist. Thus, addressing the issue of termination is part and parcel of the therapeutic process. It is just as important to end well as it is to begin well. Yet termination as a topic often receives short shrift, and as such, a number of errors of omission and commission can occur.

Error #42

Failing to Discuss Termination Early in Therapy

Failing to prepare is preparing to fail.

— John Wooden

How early in therapy should the issue of termination be addressed? For ethical and legal reasons, therapists are now advised to do so right from the beginning, informing clients of their right to terminate at their discretion. Additionally, conditions under which the therapist may terminate should be discussed. (In all cases where the therapist feels termination is necessary, referral to other therapists is essential.) There are several circumstances that can lead to the therapist and client considering termination.

1. *Lack of clinical progress*

> Claire was an alcoholic so adept at self-deception that even when she came to marital sessions inebriated she denied having a drinking problem. During these sessions she was unfocused and hostile.

The issue of not drinking before sessions was addressed to no effect. The therapist had little choice but to acknowledge that the therapy was ineffective and offer referrals for couples and individual counseling.

2. *The client's lack of willingness to participate in the therapeutic process*

Examples include frequent absences or tardiness and failure to attempt out-of-session activities. One client frequently missed sessions claiming that he "simply forgot." No form of memory enhancement such as using a palm pilot or having a friend remind him was effective. Between sessions, he never completed mutually developed assignments concerning his binge drinking and "bed hopping" (sometimes simultaneously), problems he said he desperately wanted to stop. Thus, the client was given referrals to other therapists.

3. *Recognition that the patient's treatment requires skills beyond the therapist's scope of training*

All clinicians will eventually run up against a case, fascinating as it may be, that is simply beyond their expertise (even those of us who take more than the required continuing education units and read the scientific literature dutifully). One such case involved a young woman who had joined a cult that required sterilization as part of the initiation process. She subsequently left the cult and was severely depressed and guilt ridden. Her situation was unfortunately much more complicated than tattoo removal. Appropriately, a search was conducted for a clinician who had expertise in cult recovery.

4. *Conflicts of interest*

There are many cases where conflicts of interest are obvious, such as testifying as an expert witness in a case where the lawyer is a personal friend or client. However, some cases involve more subtle issues. One such case involved a therapist who was asked by his wife to treat an old friend who had recently relocated. The therapist rightly recognized that treatment in this case would be compromised by the pressure to be especially "brilliant" and successful not only for the client's sake but for his wife's as well.

❖**Avoiding the Error**

1. The very first session can end with a summary question such as "Given what has happened here today, am I the right therapist for you to continue treatment with?" This sends a message that the client has control of the choice to continue or discontinue. Typically, clients feel empowered by such a question and rarely respond with a desire to terminate.

2. The "informed consent" form should stipulate that when either party decides to terminate the client will be asked to participate in a "summary" therapy session in which the client and therapist review the decision and the therapist provides any appropriate clinical referrals.

❖ *Error #43*

Failing to Follow Proper Termination Procedures

Just as there are appropriate intake procedures, it is necessary to have a systematic approach to the termination process as well. The termination process is not separate from the therapeutic process, and thus just as there are protocols for treatment there is a protocol for termination involving the following:

1. Discussions about termination should, if possible, be collaborative in nature as should the rest of therapy. Hopefully,

mutual decision making has been a part of the therapeutic endeavor from goal setting to out-of-session activities to treatment options. The ending of therapy should also be a process in which both parties offer their perspectives, leading to an agreed-upon plan for termination.

> Chad had essentially resolved his difficulties integrating his adult children from a previous marriage into his current family — one in which the new wife had been resistant to their inclusion. However, Chad continued scheduling sessions where little more than "shooting the breeze" was occurring. Thus, a discussion ensued in which the therapist first acknowledged that he enjoyed chatting with Chad but that he was unclear what the goal of therapy was presently. Chad replied, "For life's problems." Trying to be a good behaviorist the therapist continued by asking, "OK, can we make a list of them?" Chad then responded, "They're not that big, they come up day to day." From there the discussion gently moved to two conclusions: that these types of problems are perhaps best talked over with family, friends, pastors, etc. and that it seemed that a gradual spacing of sessions was appropriate.

2. As termination becomes imminent, time should be allotted to reflect on what the client learned and what changes in circumstance might indicate a need to return to therapy.

3. Provide the client with appropriate information regarding ongoing care. If the therapist feels that the conditions have been met to unilaterally terminate, referrals for continuous care must be made.

❖ Avoiding the Error

1. Regularly assess a client's progress. If the client and therapist feel progress is being made, such discussions can engender hope for further gains and can reinforce the therapist and client as well. If progress is stymied, facing that reality allows for corrective actions — a change of approach, inspection of alliance ruptures, or the possibility of mutual termination.

2. Consider whether a temporary break from therapy might be appropriate. To avoid a sense of abandonment, part of the "time-out" from therapy is to schedule in advance an update session to assess whether further therapy is indicated.

3. Consult with a respected colleague when deciding whether referral is appropriate.

> A therapist who knew how to treat standard impulse control behavior felt "over his head" in a case of internet pornography addiction and consulted a colleague regarding whether to refer the case. The colleague pointed out that nobody yet understood the best protocol and that his basic expertise certainly made him a good choice as therapist even though he had little experience with this specific impulse control problem.

4. Provide the client with a clear understanding of the basis for termination, and provide appropriate referrals. Again, document the proceedings of the summary session.

5. Follow up to see if the patient has continued with another therapist. Obtain a release (or a written refusal to give one) so that you can provide that therapist with input regarding the client's treatment.

❖ *Error #44*

Confusing Termination and Abandonment

There appears to be a great deal of fear on the part of therapists regarding patient abandonment. However... what constitutes abandonment is not the decision to terminate, but rather the manner in which the termination is handled....

— B. Benitez (2004)

A good termination may sound unlikely; however, endings can be framed for the client as a graduation and not as a loss. Legal and ethical complications involving client abandonment can be avoided if the following three conditions are met:

1. Having an appropriate reason for the termination.

2. Having a thorough discussion about the reasons for termination.

3. Providing the client with information regarding continuing care.

In the following case, the prerequisites for an ethical termination were not met, leading to dire consequences for the clinician.

> A therapist who had been practicing successfully for years was referred by the licensing board for supervision as part of a license reinstatement process. It seems that a client had verbally attacked the therapist, accusing her of incompetence because little progress had been made. The therapist shot back, "Well, if I am so bad, don't come back." The client didn't and went to the licensing board instead.

❖ Avoiding the Error

1. No client should ever be terminated when in the midst of crises such as those caused by divorce, trauma, and grief. This would include clients who have been hospitalized or are having suicidal thoughts.

2. Termination should never occur for the therapist's sake alone, such as when therapy is progressing well but the client is simply boring, unlikable, or slow to grasp therapeutic concepts.

3. Termination should never occur quickly, and if there is any possibility of a complaint, it should be finalized by a letter to the client with a copy placed in the file.

4. Whenever possible move toward a mutual agreement as to when therapy should end, allowing for follow-up sessions periodically if desired.

❖ *Error #45*

Failing to Be Prepared to Deal with the Myth of Time-Limited Therapy

…on close examination the research support for time limits vanishes, and the actual research evidence shows that time limits are harmful. The belief that research supports time limits has only survived because the evidence was never closely scrutinized.

— I. Miller (1996)

Those of us working within the managed care system have come face to face with a new difficulty in mental health treatment — time-limited therapy — when it is determined by an institutional review of the patient's treatment needs. Frequently, the clinician's view of the client's treatment needs is at odds with the managed care system's need for the bottom line. Thus, when doing battle with insurance companies, it is essential that therapists are familiar with the "science" (or lack thereof) behind the purported advantages of time-limited therapy (TLT).

It seems that the pendulum has swung from viewing therapy as a life-long pursuit (the Woody Allen Syndrome) to the opposite extreme where briefer is better and briefest is best. Certainly, brief therapies have been effectively applied to numerous presenting problems; however, when this is true the determination of the length of treatment was made by clinicians. That scenario is a far cry from the current situation in which managed care imposes time limits and disincentives for longer-term treatment.

So what does the research say about this issue? A multitude of studies beginning in 1956 investigated brief therapy and have been used by managed care supporters as evidence of TLT's effectiveness. However, a closer analysis of these studies by Miller (1996) reveals an astonishing lack of attention to the correct variables in many of these investigations.

For example, seven studies did in fact show that patients in short-term therapy had equivalent or better outcomes than those in longer-term treatment. However, in none of these studies were patients assigned to various lengths of treatment — the decision to end treatment was made by the therapist and/or the client. Thus, the fact that clients in short-term therapy did well is likely the result of the fact that these clients were in better shape to start with and thus required less therapy.

Miller further found that those supporting TLT have conveniently managed to ignore the fact that over 100 studies actually found a positive correlation between duration of treatment and positive treatment outcome. In addition a *Consumer Reports* survey of over 3,000 responders found that clinically determined length of therapy patients had better outcomes on all measures, including resolution of the problem, overall emotional improvement, and client satisfaction (Seligman, 1995).

Thus, there is little evidence to suggest that time-limited therapy — determined by an external agency's review of patients — is even equivalent to, let alone superior to, clinically determined length of therapy. Yet the external pressure persists.

❖Avoiding the Error

1. In cases that seem to require more therapy contact than that given by a patient's insurance company, discuss this issue with the client in advance and determine if a joint solution can be worked out. Some solutions that clients and therapists have employed successfully are
   a. A reduced session rate when insurance benefits are exhausted.
   b. Timing reimbursed sessions to end when the new insurance year begins.
   c. Spacing the time between sessions according to the client's budget and insurance benefits.

2. Explain to the client that the insurance carrier will try to spend the least possible and that the therapist has very little power in this situation since carriers have no vested interest in keeping the therapist happy (nor should they). However, managed care organizations do have an incentive to please their clients, since client satisfaction may influence whether the carrier's coverage is renewed. Thus, remind clients that they are much more influential than their therapists in receiving greater support from insurance carriers.

How to Achieve Therapist Burnout

Although each of us experiences distress differently, the literature points to moderate depression, mild anxiety, emotional exhaustion, and disrupted relationships as the common residue of immersing ourselves in the inner worlds of distressed and distressing people.

— J. L. Brady, F. L. Healy, J. C. Norcross,
and J. D. Guy (1995)

Being a therapist is largely about giving. It requires the giving of one's full and undivided attention to clients, providing abundant support and encouragement, and demonstrating unending patience and unconditional acceptance. The requirement that therapists "be there for their patients" can be rewarding but can also take an emotional toll. It is no wonder that many patients feel a lack of emotional support from their therapists. When clinicians are "emotionally exhausted," their ability to give is severely compromised.

One dire consequence of lack of self-care is therapist burnout. Maslach (1981) described burnout as a syndrome that can lead to feelings of low personal accomplishment, emotional exhaustion, and depersonalization — a state in which the therapist develops negative, cynical attitudes toward clients and clinical work. Therapists who develop burnout are at great risk for leaving the field. Thus, lack of self-care can affect every aspect of a therapist's personal and professional life.

Dr. Julie had developed expertise in the field of workers' compensation cases. Much of her workload involved being an "expert witness" in highly contested cases. Her work schedule became a nightmare as

101

she was constantly juggling unpredictable court appearances, depositions, and direct services to clients. In addition she became ever more cynical. She began to view her clients as probable "malingerers," lawyers as vicious "sharks," and judges as irrational egomaniacs. She became more irritable and depressed, withdrawing from social and recreational activities. What finally got her attention was a complaint filed with the psychology board by several attorneys she had offended. She then realized she had reached "overload" and sought treatment.

Error #46

Failing to Monitor One's Own Well-Being

One of the first assessment tools therapists use to help clients determine the sources, frequency, and types of stress they are experiencing is self-monitoring. What is good for clients is also good for their healers. Of course, clients often complain that they don't have time to chart their stress levels — and overworked therapists may use this excuse as well. In reality, if you are too busy to self-monitor, that in itself is a clear signal that you have probably reached overload.

Self-monitoring is a good first step but even more accurate information can be gathered from trusted friends, relatives, or colleagues. Therapists in a group practice often meet to discuss their cases, and this is a good opportunity to ask each other how they are feeling emotionally and energy-wise. Spouses, friends, and even children can also be tapped for their feedback as they are often the keenest observers of changes in mood or energy levels. Sometimes the input they provide is not exactly what we would like to hear — and often it is not delivered with therapist-like sensitivity. Nonetheless, those who know us best are in the best position to help us spot trouble before it escalates.

❖Avoiding the Error

1. Administer a self-assessment instrument such as the Maslach Burnout Inventory (Maslach, 1981). This instrument identifies three key components of burnout. Emotional

exhaustion describes the extent to which therapists can no longer give of themselves due to being drained emotionally. The Depersonalization subscale concerns the development of negative, cynical attitudes and feelings toward clients and clinical work. Lastly, the Personal Accomplishment subscale concerns feelings of competence and success working with clients.

2. Join or create a therapist self-supervision group. These can be formed within a group practice or through networking with your local professional association (e.g., psychologists, marriage and family therapists, clinical social workers).

3. Be vigilant for the following signs or causes of therapist overload.
   a. Seeing too many of the same types of clients.
   b. Increased irritability with clients.
   c. Decreased interest in the profession, e.g., reading journals, attendance at conferences.
   d. Increased procrastination in calling clients back or completing reports.
   e. "Back-to-back scheduling" with no breaks.

Error #47

Failing to Balance Work and Leisure

How much work is too much work? This is one area where you can trust your instincts. In the study by Maslach cited earlier, burnout was directly related to therapists' attitude toward the amount of their caseloads. Thus, if it feels like too much, it probably is. Of course, it is one thing to say, "I really need to reduce my workload." It is quite another to actually do something about it. For one thing, after having spent years building up a large and consistent referral base, downsizing is a behavioral pattern that will seem totally foreign. In addition, it is difficult to refuse to see clients who have been referred by colleagues and former patients because of concern that these sources will dry up over time if you turn down referrals.

❖ **Avoiding the Error**

1. Increase your "R and R" quotient. If there is one area in which East has met West, it is in the plethora of techniques that are now widely available to help us relax. The most well known of these are various schools of meditation, yoga, and tai chi. Of course simple muscle relaxation, imagery, and biofeedback can be as effective but lack the exotic, social, and spiritual aspects that can make Eastern approaches more appealing.

2. Avoid highly competitive recreation. Although recreational opportunities abound, it is crucial to avoid the tendency of many high achievers for recreation to become yet another realm in which to compete and excel. Thus, practicing yoga, joining a coed softball team, or going on bird watching expeditions with the Sierra Club are perhaps preferable to participation in highly competitive sports leagues and tournaments.

❖ *Error #48*

Ignoring the "Comfort Zone" of the Environment

Take a moment and look around your office space. Is it "designed by The Salvation Army?" Human beings are highly visual creatures, and the aesthetics of the work environment can contribute to our sense of well-being (not to mention that of our clients). The goal should be to create an environment in which client and therapist are made to feel at home — comfortable furnishings, a pot of coffee, attractive art work on the wall. Our workplace speaks volumes about our personalities, and silently our clients sense subtle signs of who we are. A space that is clean, organized, and patient friendly is a reflection of the clinician who inhabits that space.

❖ **Avoiding the Error**

1. Remember that many clients are highly sensitive to their environment. As one patient put it, "When my mind is messed up, the last thing I want is to be in a messy environment."

2. If you are somewhat "aesthetically challenged" do what we do when faced with tough cases — "consult" — with a professional who can create a comfortable workplace. A variety of television shows on home design have demonstrated that good taste does not have to cost a fortune, and the benefits to the human eye and spirit are priceless.

❖ *Error #49*

Overspecializing

The lives of others, their hopes, ideas, goals, aspirations, pains, fears, despair, anger — are in focus... out of the illuminated microscope we lose sight of our own needs.

— C. Rogers (1995)

A few decades ago most therapists were generalists, seeing patients with a wide array of presenting complaints. Today there are more and more specialty areas: eating disorders, domestic violence, child custody, abuse, and sexual dysfunction — to name a few. Often those who are working in these areas see clients only within their specialty. On the one hand developing an expertise is helpful in building a practice and finding a therapeutic niche. On the other hand, the lack of novelty and challenge can lead to an increased risk of burnout.

❖**Avoiding the Error**

1. Vary your clinical focus. One therapist who deals exclusively with custody evaluations volunteers at a free clinic in order to avoid overspecialization. Another way to add variety to your clinical practice is to mentor an intern or post-doctoral student.

2. The best means of self-renewal is to add diversity to your professional activities. This can be accomplished by developing and teaching continuing education seminars, becoming involving in professional organizations, and participating in research. Lastly, maybe there is a book inside you waiting to come out.

With all of the challenges facing therapists today, it is important to keep in mind that most therapists are quite satisfied with their work and would do it all over again if given the chance. Interestingly, compared to researchers, clinicians are more content with their lives and more likely to feel that their work has had a positive influence on them. Other studies have shown that clinicians feel that their work has made them better, wiser, and more aware, and has increased their capacity to enjoy life (Radeke & Mahoney, 2000). Thus, while struggling with the demands of our chosen career, we must never lose sight of the enormous benefits and privileges that accompany participation in the therapeutic endeavor.

A Final Word: The Power of Human Resiliency

❖
Error #50

Undervaluing the Power of Human Resiliency

*Most people just plain cope well.... The vast majority of people
get over traumatic events and get over them remarkably well.
Only a small subset — (five to fifteen percent) — struggle in
a way that says they need help.*

— G. Bonano (2004)

In 1998 one of the most controversial studies in the annals of
psychology was conducted. Its focus was the assessment of
the long-term mental health of those who were victims of
childhood sexual abuse. Much to the consternation of "experts"
in the field, the researchers — Bruce Rind, Philip Tromovitch,
and Robert Bauserman — found that with the exception of
father-daughter incest, when the well-being of adult victims was
compared to nonvictims, the victims had only marginally higher
levels of alcohol problems, depression, anxiety, and eating disorders.
The flack over this study, which was published in the highly
respected *Psychological Bulletin*, was so intense and widespread
that the United States Congress passed a resolution condemning
it. Nothing quite like shooting the messenger.

In spite of the results of this study and others, there is still a
fixation in the field of psychology that says, "When bad things
happen to people, there are likely to be long-term negative
consequences unless certain prescribed actions are taken that
promote healing." Translation, "When the going gets tough, the

tough should go to counseling." However, the facts do not support this view. George Bonano studied the responses of a large number of people who had recently lost a spouse. The conventional wisdom is that only by doing appropriate "grief work" can a person process and recover from such a loss; however, the opposite was found. "By far the most common response was resilience: the majority of those who had just suffered from one of the most painful experiences of their lives never lapsed into serious depression [instead they] experienced a relatively brief period of grief symptoms, and soon returned to normal functioning" (Rind et al., 1998).

The lesson here is twofold. One is that science does not always give us the answers we hoped for or expected. We must be open-minded enough to adjust our thinking and our practices when this occurs. Second, the human spirit is much more resilient than we tend to imagine. In 1974 a monumental study investigated the effect of adverse environmental factors on the development of children in Kauai, Hawaii (Werner, 1994). These were children whose parents were often alcoholic, divorced, and living in economic distress. As expected, many of these children struggled throughout their childhoods and youth with behavior problems, delinquency, and emotional problems. However, nearly as many became quite well adjusted and effective in their lives. These "resilient" children didn't require therapy to develop well, they simply required additional support growing up, such as having a grandfather or teacher who took a special interest in them.

Timothy Wilson of the University of Virginia has written that people do not always appreciate just how resilient they are. Thus when they seek out therapy, they underestimate their ability to handle adversity. As therapists, our greatest contribution may be to enhance our clients' belief in their own inner strengths, resources, and resilience.

Just as we should expect resilience on the part of our clients, so must we also recognize our own resiliency — the resilience that can enable us to face our occasional professional failings in our attempt "to understand individual patterns within the multiple patterns of the human condition — the most complicated of all species." (Skhovholt & Jennings, 2005).

Given the scope of the challenge we have undertaken, it is inevitable that we will sometimes fall short of our goals. However, as Johnny Wooden, the legendary basketball coach put it, success is not a matter of never failing, it is "... peace of mind which is a direct result of self-satisfaction in knowing you made the effort to become the best that you are capable of becoming" (Wooden, 2005).

Appendix A

Therapist Self-Assessment Questionnaire

The following questionnaire has been employed in our university graduate training program and is based on items drawn from a number of scales, including the Working Alliance Inventory. It can aid clinicians in determining whether they are addressing the major factors which affect positive therapeutic outcome. The assessment tool can be used after an initial interview with a client and periodically thereafter.

Therapist-Client Rapport

What have I said or done to ensure that the client feels liked?

How have I shown respect for my client?

When have I shown concern for my client's welfare?

How have I shown care for the client, even when the client does things I do not approve of?

Goal Clarity and Collaboration

What have I done or said to assess whether the client understands why we are focusing on specific concerns?

How have I assessed whether the client agrees with the specific goals of therapy?

How have I engaged the client collaboratively in the development of goals?

Homework

Have I provided a clear rationale for the activity?

Have I inspected barriers to the activity?

Have I used "backup" support to increase completion of the activity?

Have I reviewed non-completed assignments to determine obstacles?

Engendering Hope

What have I said or done to increase my clients sense of optimism regarding the outcome of therapy?

How have I communicated my expertise in dealing with problems such as those presented by the client?

Expectations

What have I said or done to elicit my client's expectations?

How have I clarified the client's responsibilities in therapy?

Appendix B

Asessment Instruments: Therapist Effectiveness

I. Hong Scale of Psychological Reactance

Psychological reactance, as discussed in Part IV, is the tendency to resist conformity and the influence of authority figures. It was originally proposed by Brehm (1966) as a "motivation drive directed toward the reestablishment of threatened or eliminated personal freedom." Clients who manifest such tendencies require an approach to therapy which is highly collaborative, flexible and less directive

This tool is given to the client in an early session. The means for each question are provided in parenthesis. All questions are stated so that the higher the score on each question the higher the psychological reactance.

The client is instructed to answer each question on a likert scale ranging from 1-5.

1 = never true	4 = often true
2 = rarely true	5 = always true
3 = sometimes true	

1. Regulations trigger a sense of resistance in me. (2.01)

2. I find contradicting others stimulating. (2.73)

3. When something is prohibited, I think: "that's exactly what I am going to do." (3.93)

4. The thought of being dependent on others aggravates me. (3.23)

5. I consider advice from others to be an intrusion. (3.60)

6. I become frustrated when I am unable to make free and independent decisions. (4.01)

7. It irritates me when someone points out things which are obvious to me. (3.89)

8. I become angry when my freedom of choice is restricted. (4.01)

9. Advice usually induces me to do just the opposite. (1.96)

10. I am content only when acting on my own free will. (3.23)

11. I resist the attempts of others to influence me. (3.26)

12. It makes me angry when another person is held up as a role model for me to follow. (3.60)

13. When someone forces me to do something, I feel like doing the opposite. (3.60)

14. It disappoints me to see others submitting to society's standards and rules. (2.73)

Reproduced with permission of authors and publisher from Hong, S-M, & Page, S. A psychological reactance scale: development, factor structure and reliability. *Psychological Reports*, 1989, *64*, 1323–1326. © *Psychological Reports*, 1989.

II. *The Cross Cultural Counseling Inventory — Revised*

The purpose of this inventory is to measure client perceptions about the Cross Cultural Counseling Competence of the therapist. This assessment tool is typically given to clients after the third or fourth session. The scale ranges from 1–6 with the higher scores indicating greater cultural sensitivity. The client is instructed to circle the appropriate rating under each statement.

Rating Scale: 1 = strongly disagree   4 = slightly agree
2 = disagree   5 = agree
3 = slightly disagree   6 = strongly agree

1. Counselor is aware of his or her own cultural heritage.

1   2   3   4   5   6

2. Counselor values and respects cultural differences.

1   2   3   4   5   6

3. Counselor is aware of how own values might affect this client.

1   2   3   4   5   6

4. Counselor is comfortable with differences between counselor and client.

1   2   3   4   5   6

5. Counselor is willing to suggest referral when cultural differences are extensive.

1   2   3   4   5   6

6. Counselor understands the current socio-political system and its impact on the client.

1   2   3   4   5   6

7. Counselor demonstrates knowledge about client's culture.

1   2   3   4   5   6

8. Counselor has a clear understanding of counseling and therapy process.

1   2   3   4   5   6

9. Counselor is aware of institutional barriers which might affect client's circumstances.

1   2   3   4   5   6

10. Counselor elicits a variety of verbal and non-verbal responses from the client.

    1   2   3   4   5   6

11. Counselor accurately sends and receives a variety of verbal and non-verbal messages.

    1   2   3   4   5   6

12. Counselor is able to suggest institutional intervention skills that favor the client.

    1   2   3   4   5   6

13. Counselor sends messages that are appropriate to the communication of the client.

    1   2   3   4   5   6

14. Counselor attempts to perceive the presenting problem within the context of the client's cultural experience, values, and/or lifestyle.

    1   2   3   4   5   6

15. Counselor presents his or her own values to the client.

    1   2   3   4   5   6

16. Counselor is at ease talking with this client.

    1   2   3   4   5   6

17. Counselor recognizes those limits determined by the cultural differences between client and counselor.

    1   2   3   4   5   6

18. Counselor appreciates the client's social status as an ethnic minority.

    1   2   3   4   5   6

19. Counselor is aware of the professional and ethical responsibilities of a counselor.

    1   2   3   4   5   6

20. Counselor acknowledges and is comfortable with cultural differences.

    1   2   3   4   5   6

Reprinted with permission from authors Alexis Hernandez and Teresa La Fromboise, 1983.

III. *Working Alliance Inventory*

The WAI was developed by Adam Horvath and Leslie Greenberg, based on the work of Edward Bordin (1980). A number of studies have demonstrated a significant relationship between the strength of the working alliance and positive treatment outcomes (Horvath & Greenberg, 1989). Subscales of the inventory examine whether there is agreement between the therapist and client on goals, and tasks (how to achieve the goals) and the extent of the therapist-client bond

Working Alliance Inventory — Client Short Form

The client is asked to read the following statements and provide answers on a scale from 1–7

Does Not Correspond at All		Corresponds Moderately		Corresponds Exactly		
1	2	3	4	5	6	7

1. My therapist and I agree about the things I will need to do in therapy to help improve my situation. 1 2 3 4 5 6 7

2. What I am doing in therapy gives me new ways of looking at my problem. 1 2 3 4 5 6 7

3. l believe my therapist likes me. 1 2 3 4 5 6 7

4. My therapist does not understand what I am trying to accomplish in therapy. 1 2 3 4 5 6 7

5. I am confident in my therapist's ability to help me. 1 2 3 4 5 6 7

6. My therapist and I are working towards mutually agreed upon goals. 1 2 3 4 5 6 7

7. I feel that my therapist appreciates me. 1 2 3 4 5 6 7

8. We agree on what is important for me to work on. 1 2 3 4 5 6 7

9. My therapist and I trust one another. 1 2 3 4 5 6 7

10. My therapist and I have different ideas on what my problems are. 1 2 3 4 5 6 7

11. We have established a good understanding of the kind of changes that would be good for me. 1 2 3 4 5 6 7

12. l believe the way we are working with my problem is correct. 1 2 3 4 5 6 7

IV. Assumptions About Philosophy of Human Nature Scale (PHN)

The PHN is a series of attitude statements developed by Lawrence Wrightsman (1992). Each represents a commonly held opinion, and there are no right or wrong answers. The statements are answered on a scale from –3 to +3.

If you agree strongly = +3   If you disagree slightly = –1
If you agree somewhat = +2   If you disagree somewhat = –2
If you agree slightly = +1   If you disagree strongly = –3

Scoring

The PHN has five subscales — trustworthiness, strength of will and rationality, altruism, complexity, variability, independence. Within each scale some questions are scored positively, others negatively. Below the subsets are presented with each question's means in the far right column.

Items	Men Mean	Women Mean
Trustworthiness		
Positively scored items		
2. Most students will tell the instructor when he has made a mistake in adding up their scores, even if he has given them more points than they deserved.	–0.067	–0.495
8. If you give the average person a job to do and leave him to do it, he will finish it successfully.	0.912	0.632
14. People usually tell the truth, even when they know they would be better off by lying.	–0.535	–0.609
20. Most students do not cheat when taking an exam.	0.885	1.127
26. Most people are basically honest.	1.090	1.009
32. If you act in good faith with people, almost all of them will reciprocate with fairness toward you.	1.317	1.127
38. Most people lead clean, decent lives.	0.987	0.638
Negatively scored items		
44. People claim that they have ethical standards regarding honesty and morality, but few people stick to them when the chips are down.	0.095	0.400
		(cont'd.)

Items *(cont'd.)*	Men Mean	Women Mean
50. If you want people to do a job right, you explain things to them in great detail and supervise them closely.	−0.620	−0.156
56. If most people could get into a movie without paying and be sure that they were not seen, they would do it.	0.120	0.576
62. Most people are not really honest for a desirable reason; they're afraid of getting caught.	−0.122	0.172
68. Most people would tell a lie if they could gain by it.	−0.067	0.228
74. Most people would cheat on their income tax if they had a chance.	−0.192	0.394
80. Nowadays people commit a lot of crimes and sins that no one else ever hears about.	1.057	1.371
Strength of Will and Rationality		
Positively scored items		
43. If a person tries hard enough, he will usually reach his goals in life.	1.687	1.508
49. The average person has an accurate understanding of the reasons for his behavior.	−0.852	−0.791
55. If people try hard enough, wan; can be prevented in the future.	0.397	0.462
61. The average person is largely the master of his own fate.	0.940	1.029
67. In a local or national election, most people select a candidate rationally and logically.	−0.862	−0.814
73. Most people have a lot of control over what happens to them in life.	0.927	1.237
79. Most people have a good idea of what their strengths and weaknesses are.	1.135	0.938
Negatively scored items		
1. Great successes in life, such as great artists and inventors, are usually motivated by forces of which they are unaware.	0.310	−0.026

(cont'd.)

Items *(cont'd.)*	Men Mean	Women Mean
7. Our success in life is pretty much determined by forces outside our own control.	−1.200	−1.137
13. Attempts to understand ourselves are usually futile.	−0.932	−0.723
19. There's little one can do to alter his fate in life.	−1.955	−2.146
25. Most people have little influence over the things that happen to them	−1.457	−1.394
31. Moot people have an unrealistically favorable view of their own capabilities.	−0.270	0.648
37. Moot people vote for a political candidate on the basis of unimportant characteristics, such as his appearance or name, rather than on the basis of his stand on the issues.	0.407	0.427
Altruism		
Positively scored items		
4. Most people try to apply the Golden Rule, even in today's complex society.	0.232	−0.745
10. Most people do not hesitate to go out of their way to help someone in trouble.	0.362	−0.084
16. Most people will act as "Good Samaritans" if given the opportunity.	0.510	0.348
22. "Do unto others as you would have them do unto you" is a motto that most people follow.	−0.345	−0.964
28. The typical person is sincerely concerned about the problems of others.	0.015	−0.394
34. Moot people with fallout shelters would let their neighbors stay in them during a nuclear attack.	0.425	0.140
40. Moot people would stop and help a person whose car was disabled.	0.415	−0.332
Negatively scored items		
46. The average person is conceited.	−0.022	0.218
52. It's only a rare person who would risk his own life and limb to help someone else.	0.050	0.296

(cont'd.)

Items *(cont'd.)*	Men Mean	Women Mean
58. It's pathetic to see an unselfish person in today's world, because so many people take advantage of him.	−0.452	0.182
64. People pretend to care men about one another than they really do.	0.522	0.742
70. Most people inwardly dislike putting themselves out to help other people.	−0.872	−0.283
76. Most people exaggerate their troubles in order to get sympathy.	1.030	1.228
82. People are usually out for their own good.	1.052	1.260
Independence		
Positively scored items		
45. Most people have the courage of their convictions.	0.335	0.120
51. Most people can make their own decisions, uninfluenced by public opinion.	−0.940	−0.934
57. It is achievement, rather than popularity with others, that gets you ahead nowadays. .	−0.120	0.075
63. The average person will stick to his opinion if he thinks he's right, even if others disagree.	0.367	0.055
69. If a student does not believe in cheating, he will avoid it even if he sees many others doing it.	1.777	1.348
75. The person with novel ideas is respected in our society.	0.572	0.452
81. Most people will speak out for what they believe in.	0.537	0.280
Negatively scored items		
3. Most people will change the opinion they express as a result of an onslaught of criticism, even though they really don't change the way they feel.	0.777	0.771
9. Nowadays many people won't make a move until they find out what other people think.	1.392	1.384
15. The important thing in being successful nowadays is not how hard you work but how well you fit in with the crowd.	−0.285	−0.319

(cont'd.)

Items *(cont'd.)*	Men Mean	Women Mean
21. The typical student will cheat on a test when everybody else does, even though he has a set of ethical standards.	−0.485	−0.143
27. It's a rare person who will go against the crowd.	1.105	1.465
33. Most people have to rely upon someone else to make their important decisions for them.	−0.645	−0.296
39. The average person will rarely express his opinion in a group when he sees that the others disagree with him.	0.750	0.853
Complexity		
Positively scored items		
48. I find that my first impressions of people are frequently wrong.	0.682	0.452
54. Some people are too complicated for me to figure out.	1.227	1.270
60. I think you can never really understand the feelings of other people.	−0.175	−0.068
66. You can't accurately describe a person in just a few words.	2.280	1.843
72. You can't classify everyone as good or bad.	2.465	1.892
78. Most people are too complex to ever be understood fully.	1.265	1.328
84. People are so complex that it is hard to know what makes them tick.	1.287	1.205
Negatively scored items		
6. I find that my first impression of a person is usually correct.	−0.375	−0.482
12. People can be described accurately by one term, such as "introverted" or "moral" or "sociable."	−2.127	−1.941
18. It's not hard to understand what really is important to a person.	−0.707	−0.504
24. I think I get a good idea of a person's basic nature after a brief conversation with him.	−0.130	0.400

(cont'd.)

Items *(cont'd.)*	Men Mean	Women Mean
30. If I could ask a person three questions about himself (assuming that he would answer them honestly), I would know a great deal about him.	−0.082	−0.104
36. When I meet a person, I look for one basic characteristic through which I try to understand him.	−0.485	−0.521
42. Give me a few facts about a person, and I'll have a good idea of whether I'll like him or not.	−1.007	−0.619
Variability		
Positively scored items		
5. A person's reaction to things differs from one situation to another.	2.245	2.133
11. Different people react to the same situation in different ways.	2.820	2.567
17. Each person's personality is different from the personality of every other person.	2.752	2.368
23. People are quite different in their basic interests.	1.502	1.586
29. People are pretty different from one another in what "makes them tick."	1.610	1.407
35. Often a person's basic personality is altered such things as a religious conversion, by psychotherapy, or a charm course.	0.527	0.596
41. People are unpredictable in how they'll act from one situation to another.	1.140	1.149
Negatively scored items		
47. People are pretty much alike in their basic interests.	−0.597	−0.778
53. People are basically similar in their personalities.	−1.645	−1.671
59. If you have a good idea about how several people will react to a certain situation, you can expect most people to react the same way.	−0.382	−0.234
65. Most people are consistent from situation to situation in the way that they react to things.	−0.582	−0.312

(cont'd.)

Items *(cont'd.)*	Men Mean	Women Mean
71. A child who is popular will be popular as an adult, too.	−0.430	−0.384
77. If I can see how a person reacts to one situation, I have a good idea of how he will react to other situations.	−0.557	−0.416
83. When you get right down to it, people are quite alike in their emotional makeup.	−0.905	−0.889

V. *Stages of Change Questionnaire — Sample Questions*

This questionnaire assesses a client's level of commitment to modifying a problem behavior. Lower scores on this scale correlate highly with dropping out of therapy and poorer therapeutic outcome (McConnaughy, Prochaska, & Velicer, 1983). The questionnaire is particularly useful with clients presenting with substance abuse problems.

Clients are asked to respond to the following questions on a scale from 1–4, with 1 indicating that the question is not at all true of their thinking and 4 meaning that the statement is highly characteristic.

The questionnaire is divided into four levels of commitment as indicated below. High scores on a particular question (3 or 4) indicate that the client is likely to be presenting at that level of commitment to change.

I. Pre-Contemplation Stage

1. As far as I'm concerned, I don't have any problems that need changing.

2. I'm not the problem one. It doesn't make much sense for me to be here.

II. Contemplation Stage

1. I have a problem and I really think I should work on it.

2. I'm hoping this place will help me to better understand myself.

III. Action Stage

1. I am doing something about the problems that had been bothering me.

2. Anyone can talk about changing: I'm actually doing something about it.

IV. Maintenance Stage

1. It worries me that I might slip back on a problem I have already changed so I am here to seek help.

2. I thought once I had resolved the problem I would be free of it, but sometimes I still find myself struggling with it.

Table 2, page 371, from *Psychotherapy: Theory, Research and Practice*, 1983, *20*, 368–375. Copyright © 1983 by Division of Psychotherapy (29), American Psychological Association. Reproduced with permission.

Appendix C

Assessment Instruments: Clinical Issues

Depression

Center for Epidemiologic Studies — Depressed Mood Scale (CES_D)

Radloff, L. A. (1977). A self-report depression scale for research in the general population. *Applied Psychological Measurement, 1*, 385–401.

Anxiety (Cognitive Components)

Cognitive-Somatic Anxiety Questionnaire (CSAQ)

Schwartz, G. E., Davidson, R. J. & Goldeman, D. J. (1978). Patterning of cognitive and somatic processes in the self-regulation of anxiety: Effects of meditation versus exercise. *Psychosomatic Medicine, 40*, 321–328.

Eating Disorders (Anorexia Nervosa)

Eating Attitudes Test (EAT)

Garner, D. M. & Garfinkel, P. E. (1979). The Eating Attitudes Test. An index of the symptoms of anorexia nervosa. *Psychological Medicine, 9*, 273–279.

Social Anxiety

Fear of Negative Evaluation (FNE)

Watson, D. & Friend, R. (1969). Measurement of social-evaluative anxiety. *Journal of Consulting and Clinical Psychology Bulletin, 9*, 371–375.

Post-Traumatic Stress Disorder

Impact of Event Scale (IES)

Horowitz, M. J., Wilner, N., & Alvarez, W. (1979). Impact of event scale: A measure of subjective stress. *Psychological Medicine, 41*, 209–218.

Substance Abuse (Alcohol)

Michigan Alcoholism Screening Test (MAST)

Selzer, M. L. (1971). The Michigan Alcoholism Screening Test: The quest for a new diagnostic instrument. *American Journal of Psychiatry, 127*, 89–94.

Assertiveness

Assertiveness Inventory

Alberti, R. E., & Emmons, M. L. (1974, 2001). *Your perfect right: Assertiveness and equality in your life and relationships.* Atascadero, CA: Impact Publishers.

Rathus Assertiveness Schedule (RAS)

Rathus, S. A. (1973). A 30-item schedule for assessing assertive behavior. *Behavior Therapy, 4*, 398–406.

Suggested Reading

I. HOW TO FAIL EVEN BEFORE YOU START THERAPY

Coles, D. (1995). A pilot use of letters to clients before the initial session. *Australian and New Zealand Journal of Family Therapy, 16*, 209–213.

Levilne, J. L., Stolz, J. A., & Lacks, P. (1983). Preparing psychotherapy clients: Rationale and suggestions. *Professional Psychology: Research and Practice, 14*, 317–322.

Murstein, B. I., & Fontaine, P. A. (1993). The public's knowledge about psychologists and other mental health professionals. *American Psychologist, 48*, 839–845.

Wilcoxon, S. A. (1991). Clarifying expectations in therapy relationships: Suggestions for written guidelines. *Journal of Independent Social Work, 5*, 65–71.

II. HOW TO PERFORM INCOMPLETE ASSESSMENTS

Brehm, J. (1966). *A theory of psychological reactance.* New York: Academic Press.

De Jon, P., & Miller, S. D. (1995). How to interview for client strengths. *Social Work, 40*, 729–735.

Horvath, A. T. (2003). *Sex, drugs, gambling, and chocolate: A workbook for overcoming addictions.* Atascadero, CA: Impact Publishers.

McConnauhy, E., Prochaska, J., & Velicer, W. (1983). Stages of change in psychotherapy: Measurement and sample profiles. *Psychotherapy, 20*, 368–375.

III. HOW TO IGNORE SCIENCE

Irving, J. A., & Williams, D. I. (1999). Personal growth and personal development: Concepts clarified. *British Journal of Guidance & Counselling, 27*, 517–526.

Mahoney, M. J. (1991). *Human change processes: The scientific foundations of psychotherapy.* New York: Basic Books.

Williams, D. I., & Irving, J. A. (1999). Why are therapists indifferent to research? *British Journal of Guidance and Counselling, 27*, 367–376.

IV. HOW TO AVOID COLLABORATION WITH THE CLIENT

Anderson, H. (2001). Postmodern collaborative and person-centered therapies: What would Carl Rogers say? *Journal of Family Therapy, 23*(4), 339–360.

Phillips, J. (1992). Collaboration with one's client. *Arts in Psychotherapy, 19*(4), 295-298.

V. HOW TO RUIN THE THERAPIST-CLIENT RELATIONSHIP

Alexander, L. B., Harber, J. P., & Luborsky, L. (1993). On what bases do patients choose their therapists? *Journal of Psychotherapy Practice and Research, 2*, 135–146.

Beutler, L. E., Clarkin, J., Crago, M., & Bergan, J. (1991). Client-therapist matching. In C. R. Snyder & D. R. Forsyth (Eds.), *Handbook of social and clinical psychology: The health perspective* (pp. 699–716). Elmsford, NY: Pergamon Press.

Bongar, B., Markey, L. A., & Peterson, I. G. (1991). View on the difficult and dreaded patient: A preliminary investigation. *Medical Psychotherapy: An International Journal, 4*, 9–16.

Cramer, D., & Takens, R. J. (1992). Therapeutic relationship and progress in the first six sessions of individual psychotherapy: A panel analysis. *Counselling Psychology Quarterly, 5*, 25–36.

Dorken, H., & Vandenboa, B. (1986). Characteristics of 20,000 patients and their psychologists. In H. Dorken, B. E. Bennett, L. G. Carpenter, N. Cummings, & P. DeLeon (Eds.), *Professional psychology in transition: Meeting today's challenges* (pp. 2–43). San Francisco: Jossey-Bass.

Hathcer, R. L., & Barends, A. W. (1996). Patients' view of the alliance in psychotherapy: Exploratory factor analysis of three alliance measures. *Journal of Consulting and Clinical Psychology, 64*, 1326–1336.

Mallen, M. J., Vogel, D. L., & Rochlen, A. B. (2005). The practical aspects of online counseling. *The Counseling Psychologist, 33*, 776–818.

VI. HOW TO SET IMPROPER THERAPIST-CLIENT BOUNDARIES

Gabbard, G. O. (1994). The special place of the erotic transference in psychoanalysis. *Psychoanalytic Inquiry, 14*, 483, 498.

Guthell, T. G., & Gabbard, G. O. (1993). The concept of boundaries in clinical practice: Theoretical and risk management dimensions. *American Journal of Psychiatry, 150*, 188–196.

Johnston, S. H., & Farber, B. A. (1996). The maintenance of boundaries in psychotherapeutic practice. *Psychotherapy, 33*, 391–402.

Katherine, A. (1998). *Boundaries: Where you end and I begin.* New York: MJF Books.

Mathews, B. (1980). The use of therapist self-disclosure and its potential impact on the therapeutic process. *Journal of Human Behavior and Learning, 6*, 25–29.

Satran, G. (1991). Some limits and hazards of empathy. *Contemporary Psychoanalysis, 27*, 737–748.

VII. HOW TO GUARANTEE NONCOMPLIANCE WITH ASSIGNMENTS

Kazantzis, N., Deane, F., & Ronan, K. R. (2000). Homework assignments in cognitive and behavioral therapy: A meta-analysis. *Clinical Psychology: Science and Practice, 38*(4), 365–372.

Woody, J. D. (1990). Clinical strategies to promote compliance. *American Journal of Family Therapy, 18*, 285–294.

VIII. HOW TO MAKE BAD ATTITUDES WORSE

Cooper, J., Mirabile, R., & Scher, S. J. (2005). Actions and attitudes: The theory of cognitive dissonance. In T. C. Brock & M. C. Green (Eds.), *Persuasion: Psychological insights and perspectives* (2nd ed., pp. 63–79). Thousand Oaks, CA: Sage Publications.

Holtforth, M. G., Castonguy, L. G., Borkovec, T. D. (2004). Expanding our strategies to study the process of change. *Clinical Psychology: Science and Practice, 11*(4), 396–404.

Johnson, D. (1980). Attitude modification methods. In F. Kanfer & A. Goldstein (Eds.), *Helping people change*. New York: Pergamon.

IX. HOW NOT TO CONFRONT CLIENTS

Gans, J. S., & Counselman, E. F. (1996). The missed session: A neglected aspect of psychodynamic psychotherapy. *Psychotherapy, 33*, 43–50.

Salerno, M., Farber, B. A., McCullough, I., Winston, A., & Trujillo, M. (1992). The effects of confrontation and clarification on patient affective and defensive responding. *Psychotherapy Research, 2*, 181–192.

X. HOW TO GET CLIENTS TO REFUSE MEDICATION

Biondi, M. (1995). Beyond the brain-mind dichotomy and toward a common organizing principle of pharmacological and psychological treatments. *Psychotherapy and Psychosomatics, 64*, 1–8.

Sarwer-Forer, G. J. (Ed.). (1993). Special section: Psychotherapy and pharmacotherapy. *American Journal of Psychotherapy, 47*, 387–423.

XI. HOW NOT TO TERMINATE THERAPY

Cheston, S. E. (1991). *Making effective referrals: The therapeutic process.* New York: Gardner.

Koss, M. P. (1979). Length of psychotherapy for clients seen in private practice. *Journal of Counseling and Clinical Psychology, 471*, 210–212.

Lazarus, A. (Ed.). (1996). *Controversies in managed mental health care.* Washington, DC: American Psychiatric Press.

Poelstra, P. L., & Brown, C. K. (1993). Therapeutic termination: How psychotherapists say good-bye. *Psychotherapy in Private Practice, 12*, 73–82.

Tuckfelt, S., Finkn, J., & Warren, M. (1997). *The psychotherapists' guide to managed care in the 21st century.* Northvale, NJ: Aronson.

Tryon, G. S., & Kane, A. S. (1995). Client involvement, working alliance, and type of therapy termination. *Psychotherapy Research, 5*, 189–198.

XII. HOW TO ACHIEVE THERAPIST BURNOUT

Gerson, B. (Ed.). (1996). *The therapist as a person: Life crises, life choices, life experiences, and their effects on treatment.* Hillsdale, NJ: Analytic Press.

Gilels, T. R., Prial, E. M., & Neims, D. M. (1993). Evaluating psychotherapies: A comparison of effectiveness. *International Journal of Mental Health, 22,* 43–65.

West, A. (1996). The risks of burnout. In C. Cordess & M. Cox (Eds.), *Forensic psychotherapy: Crime psychodynamics and the offender patient: Vol. 2. Mainly Practice* (pp. 229–240). London, Jessica Kingsley.

Williams, M. B., & Sommer Jr., J. F. (1995). Self care and the vulnerable therapist. In B. H. Stamm (Ed.), *Secondary traumatic stress: Self-Care issues for clinicians, researchers, & educators* (pp. 230–246). Lutherville, MD: Sidran Press.

XIII. A FINAL WORD: THE POWER OF HUMAN RESILIENCY

Blatt. S. J., Sanslow, C. A., Zuroff, D. C., & Pilkonis, P. A. (1996). Characteristics of effective therapists: Further analyses of data from the National Institute of Mental Health Treatment of Depression Collaborative Research Program. *Journal of Consulting and Clinical Psychology, 66,* 1276–1284.

Bonano, G. (2004, November 8). Human resilience. *New Yorker,* 72–74.

Curtis, R. C., & Stricker, G. (Eds.). (1991). *How people change: Inside and outside therapy.* New York: Plenum.

Masson, J. M. (1988). *Against therapy: Emotional tyranny and the myth of psychological healing.* New York: Antheneum.

Skovholt, T. & Jennings, L. (2005). Mastery and Expertise in Counseling. *Journal of Mental Health Counseling, 2,* 13–18.

Wooden, J. (2005). *Wooden on leadership.* New York: McGraw-Hill.

Bibliography

Acosta, F. X. (1980). Self-described reasons for premature termination of psychotherapy by Mexican American, Black American, and Anglo-American patients. *Psychological Reports, 47,* 435–443.

Auger, R. (2004). What we don't know can hurt us: Mental health counselors' implicit assumptions about human nature. *Journal of Mental Health Counseling, 26,* 13–24.

Barrett, M., & Berman, J. (2001). Is psychotherapy more effective when therapists disclose information about themselves? *Journal of Consulting and Clinical Psychology, 69.*

Barrett-Lennard, G. (1981). The empathy cycle: Refinement of a nuclear concept. *Journal of Counseling Psychology, 28,* 91–100.

Benitez, B. (2004). The decision to terminate therapy. *The Therapist, November/December,* 2–14.

Beutler, L., & Clarkin, J. (1990). *Systematic treatment selection: Toward targeted therapeutic interventions.* Philadelphia: Brunner/Mazel, Inc.

Bloom, B. L. (1992). *Planned short-term psychotherapy: A clinical handbook.* Boston: Allyn and Bacon.

Bonano, G. (2004, November 8). Human resilience. *New Yorker,* 72–74.

Booraem, C. D., Flowers, J. V., & Schwartz, B. (1993). Group therapy client outcome and satisfaction as a function of the counselor's use of rapid assessment instruments: As influenced by levels of computer assistance. *Proceedings of the 1992 Western Psychological Association, 72,* 135.

Bordin, E. S. (1980). *Of human bonds that bind or free.* Presidential address delivered at the meeting of the Society for Psychotherapy Research, Pacific Grove, CA.

Brady, J. L., Healy, F. L., Norcross, J. C., & Guy, J. D. (1995). Stress in counselors: An integrative research review. In W. Dryden (Ed.), *Stress in counselling in action* (pp. 1–27). Newbury Park, CA: Sage.

Brehm, J. (1966). *A theory of psychological reactance.* New York: Academic Press.

Brehm, J., & Brehm, S. (1981). *Psychological reactance: A theory of freedom and control.* San Diego, CA: Academic Press.

Castenguay, L., Goldfried, M., Wiser, S., Raue, P., & Hayes, A. (1996). Predicting the effectiveness of cognitive therapy for depression: A study of unique and common factors. *Journal of Consulting and Clinical Psychology, 65,* 497–504.

Coles, D. (1995). A pilot use of letters to clients before the initial session. *Australian and New Zealand Journal of Family Therapy 16*(4), 209–213.

Corrigan, J. D., & Schmidt, L. D. (1983). Development and validation of revisions in the Counselor Rating Form. *Journal of Counseling Psychology, 30,* 64–75.

Cross, D. G., & Warren, C. E. (1984). Environmental factors associated with continuers and terminators in adult outpatient psychotherapy. *British Journal of Medical Psychology, 57,* 363–369.

Curtis, R., Field, C., Knaan-Kostman, I., & Mannis, K. (2004). What 75 psychoanalysts found helpful and hurtful in their own analysis. *Psychoanalytic Psychology, 21,* 183–202.

Demmitt, A., & Rueth, T. (2002, March). *Challenges faced by people with personality disorders and those who counsel them or live with them.* Paper presented at the annual meeting of the American Counseling Association, New Orleans, LA.

Dormaar, J., Dijkman, C., & de Vries, M. (1989). Consensus in patient therapist interactions: A measure of the therapeutic relationship related to outcome. *Psychotherapy and Psychosomatics, 2,* 69–76.

Dowd, E. T., Milne, C. R., & Wise, S. L. (1991). The Therapeutic Reactance Scale: A measure of psychological reactance. *Journal of Counseling & Development, 69,* 541–545.

Feltham, C., & Horton, I. (2000). *Handbook of counseling and psychotherapy.* Newbury Park, CA: Sage.

Finn, S. E., & Tonsager, M. E. (1992). Therapeutic effects of providing MMPI-2 test feedback to college students awaiting therapy. *Psychological Assessment, 4,* 278–287.

Flowers, J. V., & Frizler, P. (2004). *Psychotherapists on film, 1899–1999: A worldwide guide to over 5000 films.* Jefferson, NC: McFarland & Company, Inc., Publishers.

Freeman, M., & Hayes, B. (2002). Clients changing counselors: An inspirational journey. *Counseling and Values, 47,* 13–21.

Garb, H. N. (1996). The representativeness and past-behavior heuristics in clinical judgment. *Professional Psychology: Research and Practice, 27,* 272–277.

Gitlin, M. (1996). *Psychotherapist's guide to psychopharmacology.* New York: Free Press.

Glasser, W. (2002). I can't wait until you leave. In J. A. Kottler & J. Carlson (Eds.), *Bad therapy: Master therapists share their worst failures.* New York: Bruner-Routledge.

Greenberg, L. S., & Paivio, S. C. (1997). *Working with emotions in psychotherapy.* New York: Guilford.

Hatchett, G. T., & Park, H. L. (2003). Comparison of four operational definitions of premature termination. *Psychotherapy: Theory, Research, Practice, Training, 40,* 226–231.

Heather, N., Rollnick, S., Bell, A., & Richmond, R. (1993). Effects of brief counseling among heavy drinkers on general hospital wards. *Drug and Alcohol Review, 15,* 29–38.

Hellman, I. D., Morrison, T. L., & Abramowitz, S. I. (1987). Therapist flexibility/rigidity and work stress. *Professional Psychology: Research and Practice, 18,* 21–27.

Hermansson, B. (1997). Boundaries and boundary management. *British Journal of Guidance and Counseling, 25,* 133–146.

Hong, S.-M., & Page, S. (1989). A psychological reactance scale: Development, factor structure and reliability. *Psychological Reports, 64,* 1323–1326.

Horvath, A., & Greenberg, L. (1989). Development and validation of the Working Alliance Inventory. *Journal of Counseling Psychology, 36,* 520–556.

Horvath, A. O., & Symonds, B. D. (1991). The relation between working alliance and outcome in psychotherapy: A meta-analysis. *Journal of Counseling Psychology, 38,* 139–149.

House, R. (1977). An approach to time-limited humanistic-dynamic counselling. *British Journal of Guidance & Counselling, 25.*

House, R. (1997). The dynamics of professionalism: A personal view of counseling research. *Counselling, 8,* 200–204.

Hoyt, M. F., Xenakis, S. N., & Marmar, C. R. (1983). Therapist actions that influence their perceptions of good therapy hours. *Journal of Nervous & Mental Disease, 171,* 400–404.

Hunsley, J., Aubry, T., Verstervelt, C., & Vito, D. (1999). Comparing therapist and client perspectives on reasons for psychotherapy termination. *Psychotherapy: Theory, Research, Practice, Training, 36,* 380–388.

Hynan, D. J. (1990). Client reasons and experiences in treatment that influence termination of psychotherapy. *Journal of Clinical Psychology, 46,* 891–895.

Insel, T., & Charney, D. (2003). Research on major depression: Strategies and priorities. *JAMA: Journal of the American Medical Association, 289,* 3167–3168.

Irving, J. A., & Williams, D. I. (1999). Personal growth and personal development: Concepts clarified. *British Journal of Guidance & Counselling, 27,* 517–526.

Iwanicki, E., & Schwab, R. (1981). A cross validation study of the Maslach Burnout Inventory. *Educational and Psychological Measurement, 41,* 1167–1174.

Jennings, L., Sovereign, A., & Bottorff, N. (2005). Nine ethical values of master therapists. *Journal of Mental Health Counseling, 27,* 32–47.

Johnson, D. (1980). Attitude modification methods. In F. Kanfer & A. Goldstein (Eds.), *Helping people change.* New York: Pergamon.

Karno, M., Beutler, L., & Harwood, T. (2002). Interactions between psychotherapy procedures and patient attributes that predict alcohol treatment effectiveness: A preliminary report. *Addictive Behaviors, 5,* 779–799.

Kassan, L. (1999). *Second opinions: Sixty psychotherapy patients evaluate their therapists.* New York: Aronson.

Katherine, A. (1998). *Boundaries: Where you end and I begin.* New York: MJF Books.

Kazantzis, N., Deane, F., & Ronan, K. R. (2000). Homework assignments in cognitive and behavioral therapy: A meta-analysis. *Clinical Psychology: Science and Practice, 38*(4), 365–372.

Keith-Spiegel, P., & Koocher, G. (1985). *Ethics in psychology.* New York: Random House.

Klerman, G. (1984). *Interpersonal therapy of depression.* New York: Aronson.

Klonoff, E. (1997). *Preventing misdiagnosis of women: A guide to psychiatric disorders that have physical symptoms.* Newbury Park, CA: Sage.

Frombroise, R., Coleman, H., & Hernandez, A. (1991). Development and factor structure of the Cross Cultural Counseling Inventory — Revised. *Professional Psychology: Research and Practice, 22,* 380–388.

Lambert, M. (1992). Psychotherapy outcome research. In J. Norcross & M. Goldfried (Eds.), *Handbook of therapy integration.* New York: Basic Books.

Lambert, M., & Barley, D. (2001). Research summary on the therapeutic relationship and psychotherapy outcome. *Psychotherapy: Theory, Research, Practice, Training, 38,* 357–361.

Lazarus, A. A., & Fay, A. (1977). *I can if I want to.* New York: Warner Books. Re-issued in 2000 by FMC Books, Essex, CT.

Lazarus, A. A., & Lazarus, C. (1997). *The 60-second shrink: 101 strategies for staying sane in a crazy world.* Atascadero, CA: Impact Publishers.

Lazarus, A. A. (2002). A huge dose of humility. In J. A. Kottler & J. Carlson (Eds.), *Bad therapy: Master therapists share their worst failures* (pp. 33–42). New York: Brunner-Routledge.

Mahoney, M. J. (1991). *Human change processes: The scientific foundations of psychotherapy.* New York: Basic Books.

Maslach, C. (1981). *Maslach Burnout Inventory.* Mountain View, CA: Consulting Psychologists Press.

Matross, R. (1975), Socratic methods in counseling and psychotherapy. *Dissertation Abstracts, 36 (4-b),* 1924.

McConnaughy, E., Prochaska, J., & Velicer, W. F. (1983). Stages of change in psychotherapy: Measurement and sample profiles. *Psychotherapy, 20,* 368–375.

Meyer, B., Pilkonis, P. A., Krupnick, J. L., Egan, M., Simmens, S., & Sotsky, S. (2002). Treatment expectancies, patient alliance, and outcome: Further analyses from the NIMH Treatment of Depression Collaborative Research Program. *Journal of Consulting and Clinical Psychology, 70,* 1051–1055.

Miller, W. R. (1990). Motivational interviewing with problem drinkers. *Behavioural Psychotherapy, 11,* 147–172.

Miller, I. (1996). Time-limited brief therapy has gone too far: The result is invisible rationing. *Professional Psychology: Research and Practice, 27.*

Mohl, P. C., Martinez, D., Ticknor, C., Huang, M., & Cordell, L. (1991). Early dropouts from psychotherapy. *The Journal of Nervous and Mental Disease, 179,* 478–481.

Monk, G. (1997). *Narrative therapy in practice.* San Francisco: Jossey-Bass.

Myers, W. (1982). *Shrink dreams.* New York: Simon and Schuster.

Palmer, S. E., Brown, R. A., & Barrera, M. E. (1992). Group treatment program for abusive husbands: Long-term evaluation. *American Journal of Orthopsychiatry, 62*(2), 276–283.

Pope, K., & Bajt, T. (1988). When laws and values conflict: A dilemma for psychologists. *American Psychologist, 43,* 828–829.

Prochaska, N. (2001). Stages of change. *Psychotherapy: Theory, Research, Practice, Training, 28,* 443–448.

Radeke, J. T., & Mahoney, M. J. (2000). Comparing the personal lives of psychotherapists and research psychologists. *Professional Psychology: Research and Practice, 31,* 82–84.

Reis, B., & Brown, L. (1999). Reducing psychotherapy dropouts: Maximizing perspective convergence in the psychotherapy dyad. *Psychotherapy: Theory, Research, Practice, Training, 36,* 36–38.

Rind, B., Tromovitch, P., & Bauserman, R. (1998). A meta-analytic examination of assumed properties of child sexual abuse using college samples. *Psychological Bulletin, 124,* 22–53.

Rogers, C. (1955). The necessary and sufficient of therapeutic personality change. *Journal of Consulting Psychology, 21,* 95–103.

Rogers, C. (1995). *A way of being.* New York: Mariner Books.

Sachse, R. (1990). The influence of therapist processing proposals on the explication process of the client. *Person Centered Review, 5,* 321–344.

Sealy, R. (2001). *Finding care for depression.* North York, Canada: SEAR Publications.

Seligman, M., (1995). The effectiveness of psychotherapy: The Consumer Reports study. *American Psychologist, 50,* 965–974.

Skovholt, T., & Jennings, L. (2005). Mastery and expertise in counseling. *Journal of Mental Health Counseling, 2,* 13–18.

Stokes, J., & Lauterschlager, G. (1978). Development and validation of the Counselor Response Questionnaire. *Journal of Counseling Psychology, 25,* 157–163.

Strupp, H., & Bloxom, A. (1973). Preparing lower class patients for psychotherapy: Development and evaluation of a role-induction film. *Journal of Consulting and Clinical Psychology, 4,* 373–384.

Strupp, H., Fox, R., & Lessler, K. (1969). *Patients view their psychotherapy.* Baltimore: Johns Hopkins University Press.

Sullivan, M., Skovhold, T., & Jennings, L. (2005). Master therapists' construction of the therapy relationship. *Journal of Mental Health Counseling, 27,* 48–70.

Teyber, E., & McClure, F. (2000). Therapist variables. In C. R. Snyder & R. E. Ingram (Eds.), *Handbook of psychological change.* New York: John Wiley and Sons.

Walen, S. R., DiGiuseppe, R., & Dryden, W. (1992). *A practitioner's guide to Rational-Emotive Therapy.* New York: Oxford University Press.

Wall, J., Needham, T., & Browning, D. (1999). The ethics of relationality: The moral views of therapists engaged in marital and family therapy. *Family Relations: Interdisciplinary Journal of Applied Family Studies, 48,* 139–149.

Watkins, C., & Schneider, C. (1991). *Research in counseling.* Hillsdale, NJ: Erlbaum.

Webster, M. (1991). Emotional abuse in therapy. *Australian and New Zealand Journal of Family Therapy, 12,* 137–145.

Werner, E. (1994). Children of the Garden Island. In J. S. DeLoache (Ed.), *Current Readings in Child Development* (2nd ed., pp. 1–7). Needham Heights, MA: Allyn & Bacon.

Wilkins, P. (2000). Unconditional positive regard reconsidered. *Journal of Guidance and Counselling, 28,* 23–36.

Williams, D., & Irving, J. (1999). Why are therapists indifferent to research? *British Journal of Guidance and Counselling, 27,* 367–376.

Winnicott, D. W. (1997). *Babies and their mothers.* New York: Addison Wesley.

Wooden, J. (2005). *Wooden on leadership.* New York: McGraw-Hill.

Wrightsman, L. S. (1992). *Assumptions about human nature: Implications for researcher and practitioners* (2nd ed.). Newbury Park, CA: Sage.

Yalom, I. (1997). *Theory and practice of group psychotherapy.* New York: Basic Books.

Index

The Practical Therapist Series®

Books in *The Practical Therapist Series*® are designed to answer the troubling "what-do-I-do-now-and-how-do-I-do-it?" questions often confronted in the practice of psychotherapy. Written in plain language, technically innovative, theoretically integrative, filled with case examples, *The Practical Therapist Series*® brings the wisdom and experience of expert mentors to the desk of every therapist.

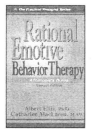

Rational Emotive Behavior Therapy
A Therapist's Guide (Second Edition)
Albert Ellis, Ph.D. and Catharine MacLaren, M.S.W., CEAP
Hardcover: $24.95   176 pages   ISBN: 978-1-886230-61-3
Up-to-date guidebook by the innovator of Rational Emotive Behavior Therapy. Includes thorough description of REBT theory and procedures, case examples, exercises.

Divorce Doesn't Have to Be That Way
A Handbook for the Helping Professional
Jane Appell, Ph.D.
Softcover: $27.95   288 pages   ISBN: 978-1-886230-71-2
Comprehensive therapist guide to divorce counseling. Emphasizes healthy, family-centered, non-adversarial approach. Key topics: understanding the divorce process, treating "problem" personalities, domestic abuse, custody, legal issues, and much more.

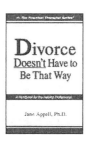

Integrative Brief Therapy: Cognitive, Psychodynamic, Humanistic & Neurobehavioral Approaches
John Preston, Psy.D.
Softcover: $27.95   272 pages   ISBN: 978-1-886230-09-5
Answers the perennial therapist question, "What do I do now?" Integrates proven elements of therapeutic efficacy from diverse theoretical viewpoints.

Defusing the High-Conflict Divorce
A Treatment Guide for Working with Angry Couples
Bernard Gaulier, Ph.D., Judith Margerum, Ph.D., Jerome A. Price, M.A., and James Windell, M.A.
Softcover: $27.95   272 pages   ISBN: 978-1-886230-67-5
The therapists' practical guide for working with angry divorcing couples, offering a unique set of proven programs for quelling the hostility in high-conflict co-parenting couples, and "defusing" their emotional struggles.

Please see the following page for more books.